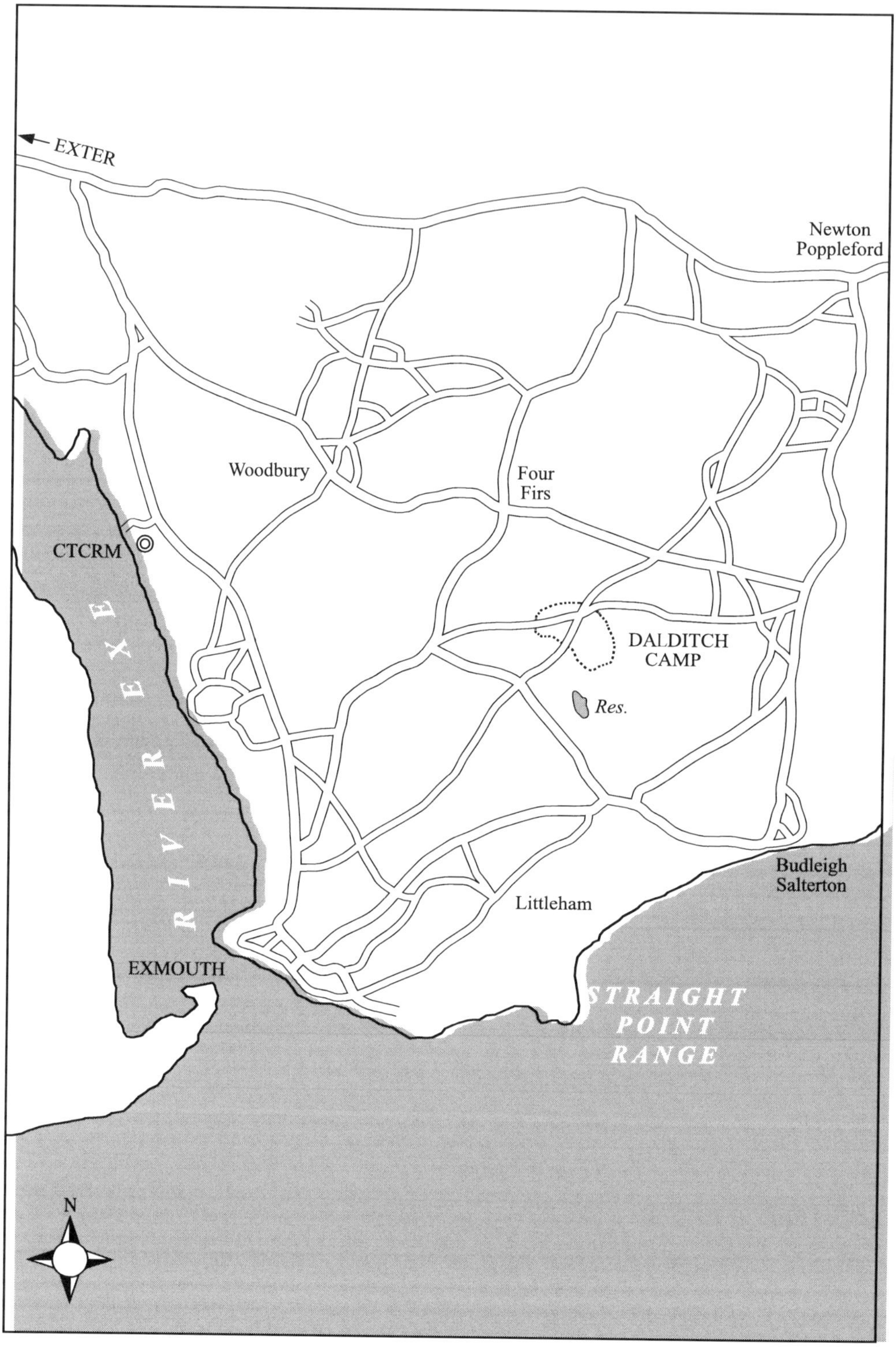

The location of Dalditch Camp in East Devon

Royal Marines in East Devon

A History of Lympstone and Dalditch Camps

Written and Edited by

Anthony John Perrett

Second Edition Series Editor

Colonel Brian Carter OBE RM

ROYAL MARINES HISTORICAL SOCIETY
SPECIAL PUBLICATION NO 8

ROYAL MARINES IN EAST DEVON
A HISTORY OF LYMPSTONE AND DALDITCH CAMPS

978 1 908123 02 2

First published 1986 by the
ROYAL MARINES HISTORICAL SOCIETY
Royal Marines Museum
Eastney
Southsea
Hants PO4 9PX
United Kingdom

Second Edition Published 2011

Printed and bound by CPI Group (UK) Ltd, Croydon, CR0 4YY

Contents

Appendices *Page*

Glossary of Illustrations

Author's Note

This publication is a revised version extracted from a complete series covering all Second World War Royal Marines camp sites within the county of Devon, which appeared in the Corps Journal *The Globe and Laurel* during 1978–80.

With a corrected and updated text, plus additional comment through correspondence to the *Globe and Laurel* Editor, it has been decided to condense all the relevant facts from several editions into this single volume, with additional illustrations.

Assistance in compiling the original facts in 1978 is gratefully attributed to Colonel D L Bailey OBE, Captain A R Lade RM, Warrant Officer Second Class G J S Offer-Hoar RM (PRO-CTCRM), the late Mr W G N Gorfin (former editor of the *Exmouth Journal*) Major A J Donald (Corps Historical Records Officer) Lieutenant J H Thomas RM, Mrs Marjorie Green, and Mr Pat Thompson (Ex-Corporal). Also acknowledged are the resources of the Corps Archives, *The Globe and Laurel* journal and the Public Records Office at Kew. (References ADM 202/113 to 119 and 120 to 123).

Additional help in updating material is attributed to Warrant Officer Second Class D Munnelly RM and Mr Robert Ridding (RMHS).

Glossary of Abbreviations

AA	'Ack-Ack'. Anti-aircraft gun fire, derived from the phonetic alphabet. Similarly 'Beer-Beer' stood for balloon barrage (Second World War).
Bde	Brigade
Bn or Battn	Battalion
CG	Commandant General
CO	Commanding Officer
Cpl	Corporal
CS	Continuous Service (regular men)
CSM	Company Sergeant Major
CTCRM	Commando Training Centre Royal Marines
EVT	Educational Vocational Training
HO	Hostilities Only (enlisted for the duration of the war)
HQ	Headquarters
IOW	Isle of Wight
ITCRM	Infantry Training Centre Royal Marines (formerly RMITC)
JE	Junior Entry
JNCO	Junior Non-Commissioned Officer
LAD	Light Aid Detachment
LUCA	Living under Canvas Allowance
MG	Machine Gun
MNBDO	Mobile Naval Base Defence Organisation
MT	Transport
MTI	Military Training Instructor
NS	National Service (post-war two years' conscription until 1963)
OC	Officer Commanding
OCTU	Officer Cadet Training Unit
OOD)	Officer of the Day (Duty Officer)
PA & Defence	Passive Air Defence
POW	Prisoner of War
PT	Physical Training
QM	Quartermaster
Rct	Recruit

RHU	Reinforcement Holding Unit
RMB	Royal Marine Band
RMRD	Royal Marine Reserve Depot
RMTG (D)	Royal Marine Training Group – Devon
RMTG (W)	Royal Marine Training Group – Wales
RNVR	Royal Naval Volunteer Reserves
Royals	Royal Marines (a nickname)
RT	Recreational Training
SA (Ranges)	Small Arms
Sgt	Sergeant
SL Rgt	Searchlight Regiment
SNCO	Senior Non-Commissioned Officer (Sergeant and above)
SR	Special Reservist
TEWT	Tactical Exercise without Troops
Trg or Tg	Training
UIF	Unit Institute Fund
YO	Young Officer

42 Commando Trooping the Colour at Lympstone 6 May 1955
(The Tenth Anniversary of VE Day)

Part One

RM Reserve Depot

Exton

RM Reserve Depot – Exton

Mobilisation

During the summer of our discontent in 1939, as war clouds gathered and the Conscription Act passed in June held all young men aged over twenty-one years in a state of tension, Senior Officers of the Royal Marines, and other interested persons, finalised their plans for the building of a Special Reserve Depot. Tankerton, on the north Kent coast, had been suggested as a possible site, and also Littleham on east Devon's coastline, between Exmouth and Budleigh Fullerton. Instead the choice finally favoured the historic Nutwell Court Estate just north of Exmouth on the eastern bank of the River Exe, on land owned by descendents of Sir Francis Drake.

Why Tankerton and Littleham should have proved unsuitable I cannot say, for my original theory that the latter was discredited by Their Lordships for fear of disturbing the eternal rest of Lady Nelson lying buried in the village churchyard was dashed on finding out that Straight Point firing range was set up on the presumed camp site shortly afterwards! Whatever the reasons, I feel confident that all who have sampled the delights of the modern Commando Training Centre at Lympstone that has emerged from the ruins of the old Exton camp will agree that the creators chose well.

The area selected to be segregated from the remainder of the Drake Estate formed a large part of the Lower Nutwell Farm. Land preparation commenced well before the declaration of war on 3 September, and its first intended inmates assembled at Eastney Barracks as the 'RM Special Reserve' on 12 October under the care of Major G W M Grover RM during their Portsmouth lodging, whilst the Commanding Officer, Lieutenant Colonel C R W Lamplough RM was detained on urgent work at the Admiralty. The first 250 militiamen soon swelled to 400 as the 'intake machinery' geared into action, undertaking a six weeks' disciplinary course (Hostilities Only 1–10 Squads) which they completed by the end of November, the majority being turned over to the Mobile Naval Base Defence Organisation for Anti-aircraft Artillery, whilst their still warm beds were quickly filled by the second 400 (Hostilities Only 11–20 Squads) who occupied them until 26 January in the new year. The first six of these squads also went to the Mobile Naval Base Defence Organisation and the other four remained at Eastney to form part of the RM Brigade, whilst one man from this entry achieved notoriety as 'the Marine who never was' for a Marine Murray reported sick on the day of joining at Eastney was rushed to Haslar Hospital for an emergency operation and was thence discharged without ever having been in uniform or slept in a barrack bed!

The Move to Devon

Now Devon beckoned even though the camp site was nowhere near ready, the severe winter ice and snow conditions having held up the first bricklaying for two months. Permanent staff had begun assembling there since November and were billeted in Exmouth or villages of the surrounding area, being collected in lorries each morning and returned later in the day. On 22 February 1940 the first trainees arrived and were greeted by Lieutenant Colonel Lamplough the Commanding Officer, who had been released from the Admiralty since November to supervise the building programme, and with them came Corporal A P Thompson, a recalled pensioner who had completed his full twenty-one years in 1937. He was to become The Globe and Laurel's correspondent for the next two years as a staff member and in his introductory writing offered at first the only clue to the location of this future nursery of the corps as '… somewhere in the heart of the country (south) on the banks of the River E, where the soil is red clay and a railway station lies nearby'. Well I'm sure that fooled nobody, and least of all the Germans, who, if they did not already have their agents in position, might easily have learned from any self-respecting historian that their Saxon ancestors made settlements at Woodbury and Exeter (Exanceaster) by the attraction of this same fertile red soil in the eighth century! What did cause some confusion perhaps was the subsequent renaming of that railway station from 'Woodbury Road' to 'Exton' while the camp which had originally taken its name from that hamlet later associated itself with the next village along – 'Lympstone' –and had another village, 'Topsham' for it's telephone number!

Corporal Pat Thompson, the Globe and Laurel reporter/photographer, in his office and on the move

Albert (Pat) Thompson recalls that they left Eastney under great secrecy and were at first also billeted in with local families, leaving their comfy digs to fill up each wooden hut in camp as it was completed and furnished with new pattern white enamel kit lockers, chairs, tables, and beds etc (both single and double bunk variety with white naval counterpanes). Despite the many trials and tribulations experienced during this protracted building period the recruits were said to be much impressed with their quarters when they moved in, remarking on the constant supply of hot water available, and although this last facility has been disputed as 'propaganda' by some reminiscing former inhabitants recently there can certainly be no doubt over the chaos outside the huts where unmade roads were mud tracks and the whole site was littered with pipes, cables, tractors, steamrollers and such like paraphernalia. During those early months there was no Sick-Bay, Gymnasium, or Drill Shed, and only the smallest of parade grounds… which no doubt helped to give recruits that professed good impression! A newly completed garage belonging to Standfield and White Limited on the A30 Honiton Road just outside of Exeter was commandeered as a store for all the camp equipment, under RM Guard, until being relinquished at the end of June, by which time the greatly improved climatic conditions had permitted building progress to leap ahead.

A typical hut in 1940

The parade picture in the Daily Mirror, *7 March 1940*

Number Two Dining Hall (note Marines wearing seamen's white fronts)

Each hut contained two or three coke-fired stoves, with an additional one in the SNCO's cabin at the end, and covered walkways connected to the ablution rooms which were 'tastefully' decorated in brown (top) and cream (bottom) restful colours! Recruits at this time were attending lectures and church services in Number Two Dining Hall (a trifle confusing as there was only one built at this stage!) and concerts were given in the canteen during the springtime.

Lieutenant Colonel Lamplough's stay at Exton proved short, for on 4 February that first year he was recalled to the Admiralty and handed over the camp to Lieutenant Colonel F W Dewhurst RM, whose subordinates included Captain C F Phillips (Commandant), Sergeant Major 'Jumper' Cross and QMS (Barrack) Jewell.

Recruit Squads

Marine Smith-Howell from Sussex was recorded as the first 'client' to sign in at this establishment, although it is extremely doubtful that he was actually the first to pass through the simple barrier at the main gate, spending his first day in joining routines and kitting up.

Kit Layout

According to my calculations, of the first 360 lads brought down from Eastney on 22/23 February (21–28 Squads) only 320 were left by the completion of their training, and these were posted to 101 RM Brigade at Bisley. The public were treated to a glimpse of these men at work when a full page of the *Daily Mirror* for Thursday 7

March featured them in text and photographs as 'Britain's great hope' although the camp was not named of course due to censorship. The normal six weeks' course covered the basics of fieldcraft, weapon handling, physical training and drill, so that those in need of specialised training went on to other centres.

29 Squad seems to have disappeared without trace (if it existed), for the next recorded were 30–40 who came direct to the RM Reserve Depot during the three days of 9–11 April, and totalling 550 formed the largest intake; but after only two weeks a number of them were sent immediately for Sea Service training, leaving the remainder reformed into 30–37 Squads to pass for duty on 25 May. At this stage it was decided that Hostilities Only recruits should be reclassified; Exton Hostilities Only men were to be sent for sea service, to differentiate from Hostilities Only recruits trained at the Divisions, therefore HO 38 Squad became HOX 1 and so on. HOX 1 and 2 went to Chatham for sea service, HOX 4 and HOX 5 to Portsmouth for similar duties, and HOX 7 and HOX 8 went to Plymouth ships, leaving HOX 3 and HOX 6 to join the Mobile Naval Base Defence Organisation (the latter claiming they were the unlucky ones!). This 'X' factor in Squad numbering should not be confused with that attached to Divisional Numbers. 'X' was added to the divisional prefix in October 1925 to denote men re-entered under revised rates of pay after a break of less than five years. A new series starting from 'one' reached four figures when the practice ceased in 1948 (although the Band Service continued to use the 'X' until august 1955). In wartime the original HO entries bearing EX prefix changed on reaching four figures to CH/X, PLY/X, PO/X and RMB/X with six figures, whilst Continuous Service men remained in the four figure series.

By this time the gymnasium was completed, the cinema/theatre was taking shape, with the church dwarfed between the two …and 400 copies of *The Globe and Laurel* were sold in the camp that month!

Elsewhere on the war front, Poland, Norway, Denmark, Holland, Belgium and Luxemburg had been overrun by the Germans, HMS *Royal Oak*, a major battleship, had been tragically sunk at Scapa Flow and retaliation came with the enemies' forced scuttling of their prime ship *Graf Spee* in the River Plate; whilst even as HO 30–37 Squads were dispersing from Exton for their various duties on 25 May orders were being despatched to France for the commencement of the great Dunkirk evacuation that would end on 4 June, with the subsequent fall of that country on 23 June leaving Britain virtually alone and threatened with her own invasion… Things could hardly have been worse, but what country doesn't have its little ups and downs?

Under the powers of the National Service Act passed by Parliament, HM the King signed a proclamation on 1 January 1940 conscripting an estimated eligible 2,000,000 men between the ages of nineteen to twenty-eight, and this was followed by another signed on 9 May raising the age to thirty-six. Later on it was deemed necessary to revise this to eighteen to forty-one years, eventually reaching fifty-one years for males

The 'Sylvan Glade' (the office on the right still stands).

and unmarried females between twenty and thirty – business was becoming brisk at Exton! Thus it proved necessary to expand and take in the field opposite the main gate (sports grounds today) from the beginning of May for use as a tented site, and this was first occupied by units of the Mobile Naval Base Defence Organisation on 10 May, to be joined on 15 May by the 11th Searchlight Regiment HQ and 'S' Battery (prior to moving to Andover). Then also came the 1st RM (H) Anti-aircraft Regiment, making quite a large canvas annex. These men used the main camp ablutions and other amenities, eating in the main dining hall in advance of the Depot meal times, and fortunately enjoyed good weather and plenty of sport.

All of the old 45–49 Squads (now HOX 8–12) went for Sea Service in the divisions after initial training, as did HOX 13–19, recruited 30–31 May (of whom we know that half were volunteers) with the exception of HOX 17 who went to London for Admiralty Guard duties: and due to their employment in preparing suitable defences around the camp the men of these five squads had their stay at Exton extended by a week as compensation to complete the curriculum, passing for duty at the end of July. They were the last of the renumbered squads; for the next batch HOX 20 and onwards joined directly in the X category.

Deal Temporarily Indisposed

Meanwhile, across at Deal in Kent (nicknamed 'Hellfire Corner') things were getting a bit too hot to handle being on the direct bombing run to London as well as coming within shelling range of Calais, thus was the depot hastily vacated by all but a Holding Battalion of caretakers. Continuous Service squads 390 and 391 moved out on 1 July, to continue their training at Exton, occupying the tented camp recently emptied by the Anti-aircraft and Searchlight Regiments, preceded on 30 May by the boys of the School of Music under their senior assistant musical director Lieutenant A C Green. They had travelled down on a special train, and moved into 'A' Company huts in the main camp, messing in Number One Dining Hall and receiving instructions at the Gun Battery. The Military Instructors Unit and NCO's School also came along as did the new Commanding Officer for the Royal Marine Reserve Depot, Brigadier A P Dawson, to succeed Lieutenant Colonel Dewhurst RM, plus Major E Bowling RM and many other officers, NCOs and men of the Deal Staff... and to complete the complement the first three Wrens to enter the all male Exton domain! One of these, Wren Patterson, (now Mrs J Snowden) is a member of the Royal Marines Historical Society.

The Band Boys had come to continue their training in a comparatively safe area, learning to become proficient on two instruments; woodwind or brass for the Military Band, and stringed instruments for the Orchestra (although solo instrumentalists played in both), many of them learning also to play dance band instruments. In addition the boys continued their education under the Headmaster, Captain Grey, and the schoolmasters from Deal were there in full force; there was military training, Physical and Recreational Training sessions and First Aid instructions; then when the boys were free of all these duties, they acted as Cyclist Orderlies and stretcher bearers for the Passive Air Defence organisations.

Soon it was realised that, as more men were called up: the boys would be taking up too much room at the Depot, so efforts were made to find suitable accommodation for both wings of the School of Music to be together again. The Seniors, having moved to Plymouth, had practice rooms in the dungeons of an old fort, administration in an old stable block and the music room in a disused chemical laboratory; a small piece of waste ground was used for parades, and the men were in billets, so the Admiralty made a special camp at Malvern for the complete School of Music. Ten months later this was taken over by the Navy as a 'stone' frigate (HMS *Duke*), and once more the school had to be split up; the junior wing to Howstrake Holiday camp on the Isle of Man, and the seniors to the Clifton and Norbreck hotels at Scarborough. Then, in the late summer of 1946, a former American Army camp at Bedford, Oxfordshire brought the two wings together once again, remaining there until January 1950, when they returned to Deal. Exton Camp had its own twenty-strong band of RN School of Music Pensioners since 29

March under Band Sergeant E King, but in the continual game of 'musical chairs' even the 'old and bold' moved on a month after the boys, headed for Wales, and in their place soon after came Band Sergeant Wally Smith's twenty-four musical pensioners (average age forty-six years) from the Divisional Bands.

Still in the field of entertainment, the Globe Theatre had it's grand opening night one Sunday in July 1940 when Recruit Greenwood's piano recital was followed by a cartoon film, then the main feature; thus was a whole wonderful new spectrum open to them… even if there was only one projector for the first month and the story line (not to mention the audiences patience) waned at times! Programmes changed thrice weekly, and when the silver screen was not in use action continued on the stage with the 'illustrious boards' being trodden by 'home-grown' as well as ENSA artists; the first big concert was in October when the entire second half, lasting an hour, featured 'The Loonies', a section of the band, attired in fancy dress, under their leader, Leading Looney Perratt! The succeeding years brought some notable stars that included Anna Neagle, Claude Hulbert, 'Coco' the Bertram Mill's Circus clown, and actor Hugh Williams who, in the fourth year, brought his successful play 'Claudia' down from London following a two-year run at the St Martin's Theatre. It was a 'captive' if not 'captivated' audience, for little leave was given to the recruits until the completion of the six weeks training.

The Cinema/Theatre

Although perhaps not in the 'entertainments' category but at least next door, the Church of St Albans opened at about the same time as the theatre or, as they say in the profession, was 'dedicated' by the Chaplain to the Fleet the Venerable Archdeacon T Crick CBE MVO MA KHC RN for the Reverend Leonard Coulshaw MC AKC and E Williams to house their respective flocks.

As entertainments officer, Major Hugh Frossard provided films or stage shows every night. Here he sits on the left of 'Miss England' (1944).

The Church

Meanwhile, CS 390 Squad had passed for duty to Chatham on 10 August with CS 391 following on four days later to Portsmouth, and the tented camp, now vacated, was struck on 27 August (all other CS Squads trained at the divisions). With Deal drastically contracted, Exton then assumed the Depot role although it was not until October 1941 that *The Globe and Laurel* actually referred to it as such (RM Depot Devon), as prior to this it variously went under the guise of RMRD (Devon) or RMRD (Exmouth) and (Exton).

The layout of the camp in 1940 was that on entering the main gate and passing down the main road, the guardroom, Commanding Officer's office and Headquarters offices were on the right hand side, and behind these were the officers' accommodation huts, the Officers' Mess, Sick-bay and Dental Block. The Gymnasium, and cinema/theatre were situated further down, below Sylvan Glade while the Company Offices, Senior Non-Commissioned Officers Mess, Recruit Lines, main galleys and stores were all to the left.

In June anti-invasion defences were built around the camp, to be manned by recruits.

Heeding the government's appeal to the country to 'dig for victory', the Exton men turned the spaces between their huts into vegetable gardens, vying with each other for competitive produce that found it's way into the cookhouse.

Change and Completion

Command of the Reserve Depot changed hands once again in this first year, passing from Brigadier A P Dawson to Brigadier N K Jolley OBE on 29 September, but as he was also Commander of 103 RM Brigade now seeking temporary accommodation at Exton, the administration of the Depot passed to Lieutenant Colonel M H Spicer RM for the time being. Training intakes were thus curtailed for about three months whilst these lodgers took up residence so that by the end of the year there were only three squads left occupying 'A' and 'B' Lines, the 7th Battalion having taken over 'C' and 'D' Lines as squads completing training moved out: and the 8th Battalion 'F' and 'G' Lines.

So it was a rather mixed bag of lads who sat down to Exton's first Christmas dinner of lentil soup, roast turkey, baked potatoes, sprouts, parsnip, Christmas pudding and white sauce, followed by afternoon tea consisting of pineapple and custard with Christmas cake and mince pies, then supper offering cold ham and pickles... a somewhat sumptuous menu one might think for a besieged country facing bleak prospects; the resultant product of course depending on the state of the cooks at the time!

Barely were the festivities over however when 103 Brigade were broken up, mostly to reinforce the Mobile Naval Base Defence Organisation now ordered overseas, but leaving those under-age and permanent staff of the 7th Battalion to find other billets at the RM Division Reinforcement Depot (Hayling Island), while 8th Battalion staff moved westward to the Thurlestone Hotel near Kingsbridge to prepare an Officer Cadet Training Unit for future young RM officers.

Now the way was clear for Exton to get down to its real business again and from 22 January 1941, recruit intakes rapidly built up to about thirty squads at any one time (hitting a peak of thirty-four in one instance) with around forty men per squad. To provide enough instructors for this sudden inrush it proved necessary to second eighteen Junior Non-Commissioned Officers from the 7th and 8th Battalions to fill the breach, seven getting their own squads whilst the remainder acted as 'rear rank instructors'.

By the summer of 1941 the camp was really taking shape, with trimmed lawns and vegetable plots growing to such profusion that the first of several annual 'Horticultural Shows' was held to raise money for charity, with the camp's hay crop yielding an estimated £180 towards it; and just to prove that war was not 'all work and no play' they held their first public sports day, between showers, on 16 August. Not until two years after its inception however could we report in February 1942 that Royal Marine Reserve Depot was complete to do its original plan, with made-up roads and all 'ship-shape'. Some of the larger buildings such as the Gymnasium, theatre and workshops were entirely of brick construction, but the majority were of wood and

A first public (possibly horticultural) day at Exton Camp

metal on concrete foundations, and this included the Officers' and Sergeants' Messes as well as all the accommodation huts. Sergeant Major R J Ashby held the first post as President of the SNCOs' Mess which functioned almost from the very beginning, as did a JNCOs' Club.

Some Leave Their Mark

The original reservists had been given the prefix SR to their service number, later changed to EX for Exton to differentiate from the three divisions; Chatham (CH), Portsmouth (PO) and Plymouth (PLY), but this practice ceased in October 1940 when they reverted to Divisions again. The relatively few who were allotted EX numbers started in three figures and ended in four, and the man who by chance drew EX 1664 (the year of the corpse formation) was Marine Alfred John Hider who, on joining in February 1940, went on to serve in Crete, Egypt, Ceylon and Normandy and, although surviving the war, the experience obviously 'drove him literally to drink', for his employment after demob was as a manager of a wine merchant's branch!

Undoubtedly the most famous recruit to pass through this establishment, however, did not survive the ravages of war unfortunately. He arrived almost unnoticed on Tuesday morning 23 June 1942 at Woodbury Road Station (Exton) after an all-night journey from Edinburgh and was just 'one of the crowd' with a number – CH/X 110296 – allotted, that was of no significance at the time. Completing training on 10 August this eighteen-year-old lad passed to 20th Training Battalion and thence on to the 2nd Battalion on 9 October. From his camp on the Isle of Wight he made countless training landing assaults in the Southampton area before the Battalion reformed as 43 Commando and went through the 'dreaded Achnacarry Course' in August 1943; from there he went, via Algeria and Tunisia, to an untimely death at a then little known place called Comacchio in Italy on 2 April 1945, as war in Europe was drawing to a close. The name Thomas Peck Hunter lives on however with the memorial bell dedicated to him a year later in the camp that trained him, as the only Corps Victoria Cross holder of that war, and on display just inside the main gate. His twenty-one-year life span began in Aldershot, and after

Corporal Thomas P Hunter VC

Officers' Mess huts

A partial aerial view of the camp, showing the railway line

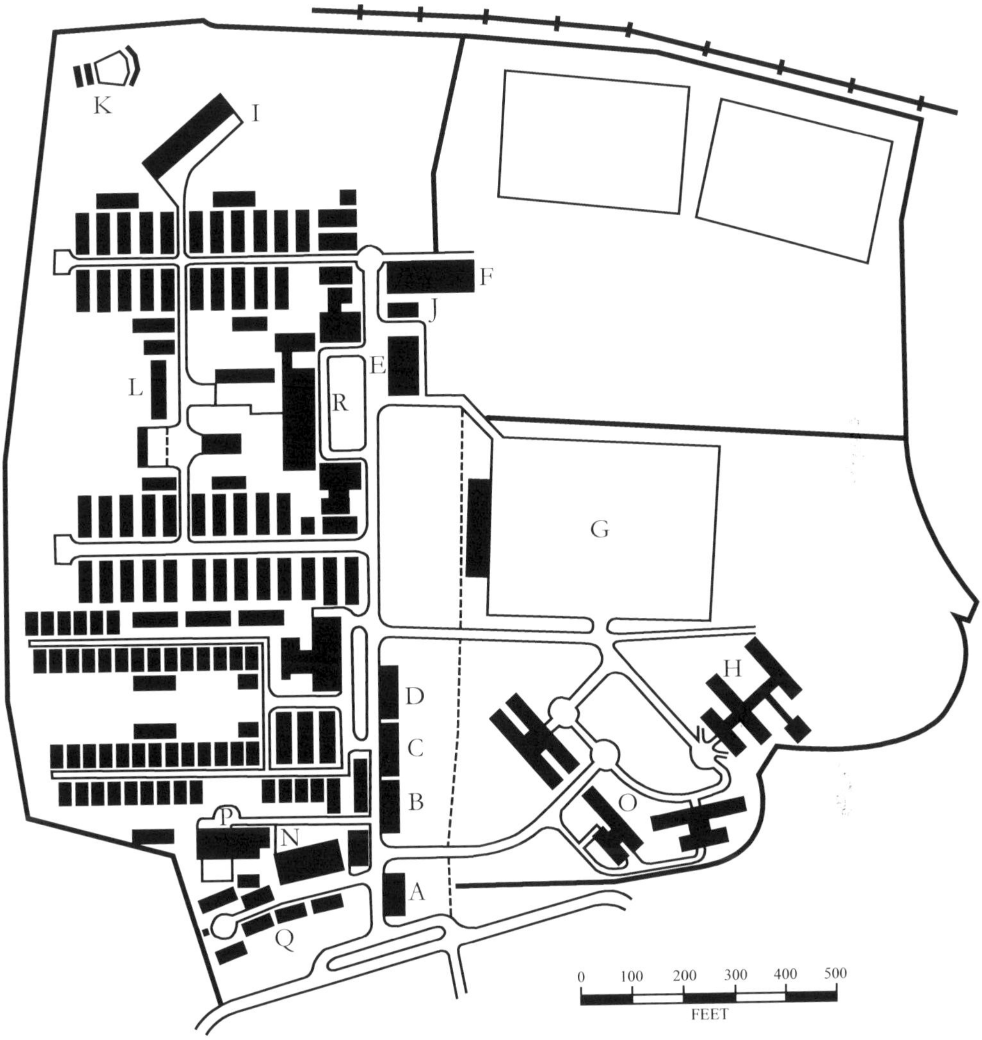

A	Guardroom	J	Church
B	Pay Office	K	30yd Range
C	Staff Office	L	Miniature Range
D	Quartermaster's Office	N	Garage
E	Theatre	O	Officer's Mess
F	Gymnasium	P	Sergeant's Mess
G	Parade	Q	Stores
H	Hospital	R	Recreation Room
I	Gun Battery		

Layout of the original Lympstone Camp

The original location of the 'Hunter Bell', later resited

schooling in Tynecastle and Stenhouse took up a peacefull vocation as a stationer with Waddle and Co Limited in Edinburgh; a single man still when he died, Hunter made the rank of Lance Corporal on 6 October 1943 and Temporary Corporal in his last month.

But before this all happened a new development was taking shape nearer home; more important than the arrival of a further twenty Wrens under Leading Wren Ferguson's care in September 1941, or the fact that one of them, Guy by name, was shortly to marry the Padre (Reverend L Coulshaw) and also by the end of that year oust our correspondent Corporal Thompson from his cushy administrative job to the more rigorous task as first warden of Straight Point Range. More important even than that the said corporal had managed to sell 600 of the total 6,200 *Globe and Laurel*s produced at the time of his departure, or the fact that in September Brigadier A P Dawson had returned to command the Depot once again!

Previously, apart from specialised grades such as the 'All Norton Drivers and Mechanics Squad' (HOX36) and 'Cooks, Clerks and Drivers' (HOX57 and 70), plus the usual quota of Signallers etc going on advanced training elsewhere, the bulk of the men had passed for duty either to one of the divisions, the Beach Engineering Battalion at Havant, or the newly formed MNBDO 11 at Hayling Island's 'Sunshine Camp'; now, as Tom Hunter appeared on the scene, they were marching out of Exton, led by the Staff

Band and with the Commandant taking the salute outside his office (as he did on every occasion no matter the time of day), down narrow deserted country lanes just a few miles to Dalditch.

Note: At this stage the new khaki 'battle dress' was replacing the khaki 'service dress' (compare photographs on pages 18 and 22). This rough serge 'ginger suit' which buttoned right up to the neck looked rather ungainly compared to the smarter 'open-neck with tie' version that superseded it in 1948. Best blue serge uniforms would only be in the possession of permanent staff (Continuous Service) but those recruits who passed for duty on Sea Service would draw utility blue dress and working uniforms at their respective divisions (this wartime tunic did not have bottom pockets, and the two top ones were unpleated). The headgear in vogue at the time was the khaki field service cap; the blue beret not making an appearance at Exton until late 1943, and the green one well after the war.

The first three wrens (Jerram, Patterson and Fishe) with the MTI staff

Admiral of the Fleet Sir Roger Keyes with the Zeebrugge NCOs.
Rear row (*left to right*): CSgt Douglas, CSgt Rookes, CSgt Tracey.
Front row (*left to right*): QMS Knill, CSgt Burnell, Sgt Kingshott, Sgt Aylward, QMS Burt.

Part Two

RM Infantry Training Centre

Dalditch Camp

On parade at Dalditch

RM Infantry Training Centre – Dalditch Camp

Searching for Dalditch Camp today is like undertaking an archaeological survey of some ancient civilisation, for much of the remains lie buried in the tangled undergrowth of East Budleigh Common, leaving just a few traces of red brick walls, concrete foundations and steps. Apart from the rifle range walls in the southeast corner of this Second World War site, only four of the original buildings remain; a solidly constructed garage plus three decontamination centres, one of which is open to view: another partially so: but the third entirely encased by creepers. Provided with an original map, photographs and a vivid imagination it is possible to mentally reconstruct this camp.

Location

The camp took its name from a minute hamlet half a mile distant that consists of only about six dwellings, a farm, and livery riding stables which I understand were utilised by Corps Officers at the time. A further quarter mile down this valley comes the slightly larger community of Knowle which boasts one public house – the Britannica – run then, as now, by Olive Doney, a lady who well remembers the camp and her few regular customers – mostly of the permanent staff. The young trainees preferred to trek the couple of miles into either East Budleigh or Budleigh Salterton, then gratefully clamber aboard trucks for the uphill return trip; whilst the more adventurous took themselves off to the metropolis of Exmouth some four miles distant.

It was to the peaceful little Knowle that Corporal W Turner brought his wife for a quiet weekend break from the Portsmouth blitz during his camp building programme, only to be greeted by a stick of bombs being dropped across the village by a stray German aircraft! This was probably the same enemy plane that Corporal A P Thompson, the Straight Point range warden spotted, and following his urgent telephone call to the local RAF airfield it was last seen disappearing into the sea off Teignmouth with a Spitfire on its tail. I have had no other reports of bombing raids on either Exton or Dalditch camps, although Exeter of course suffered terrible damage, and to a lesser degree Exmouth also. This is all the more surprising in the case of Dalditch on learning that an urgent signal was sent by the War Office to the Commanding Officer there ordering a check on its vulnerability from the air, and a reconnaissance aircraft reported that the camp was entirely visible whilst flying above Exeter. Attempts were then made to try and camouflage the site.

Comparisons, Construction and Complications

Dalditch differed in many ways from its neighbour RM Reserve Depot Exton; firstly it was built on 'common' instead of 'private' land and commenced as a tented encampment (remaining a mixture after huts were erected) whilst Exton (as we saw in Part One) rose directly out of the farmland mud, having 'boxed' wooden huts in contrast to the semicircular corrugated 'Nissen Huts' of Dalditch, so named after their designer Colonel P N Nissen (1871–1930), although the accommodation layout within was similar in both types and heating came from enclosed coke stoves.

Nissen hut interior

So many units passed through this camp, of varying durations, that not only is it possible to miss a few but space prohibits a comprehensive detail here anyway, and amongst the earliest, if the information contained in the Exton Photograph Album in the Corps archives is correct, were recruits of X110 and X111 squads who, passing for duty on 1 May 1941 claim to have been the first to march out to Dalditch; but if this is so they must have trailed their tents behind them for certainly no permanent structures appeared before that July, and the first four huts erected (approximately 100 yards east of Four Firs X-Roads) were occupied by Corporal Turner and his men who built them! Four Firs was not destined to form part of the main camp site however, although it was used as a training area, tank circus, and many men lived here under canvas; the selected tract of heartland started about half a mile northwards and divided into five sub-areas known as 'Frying Pans', 'Tuckers', 'Triangle', 'Hayes' and 'Wheathill' covering a vaguely rectangular section a good mile in length to half a mile in breadth at its widest point.

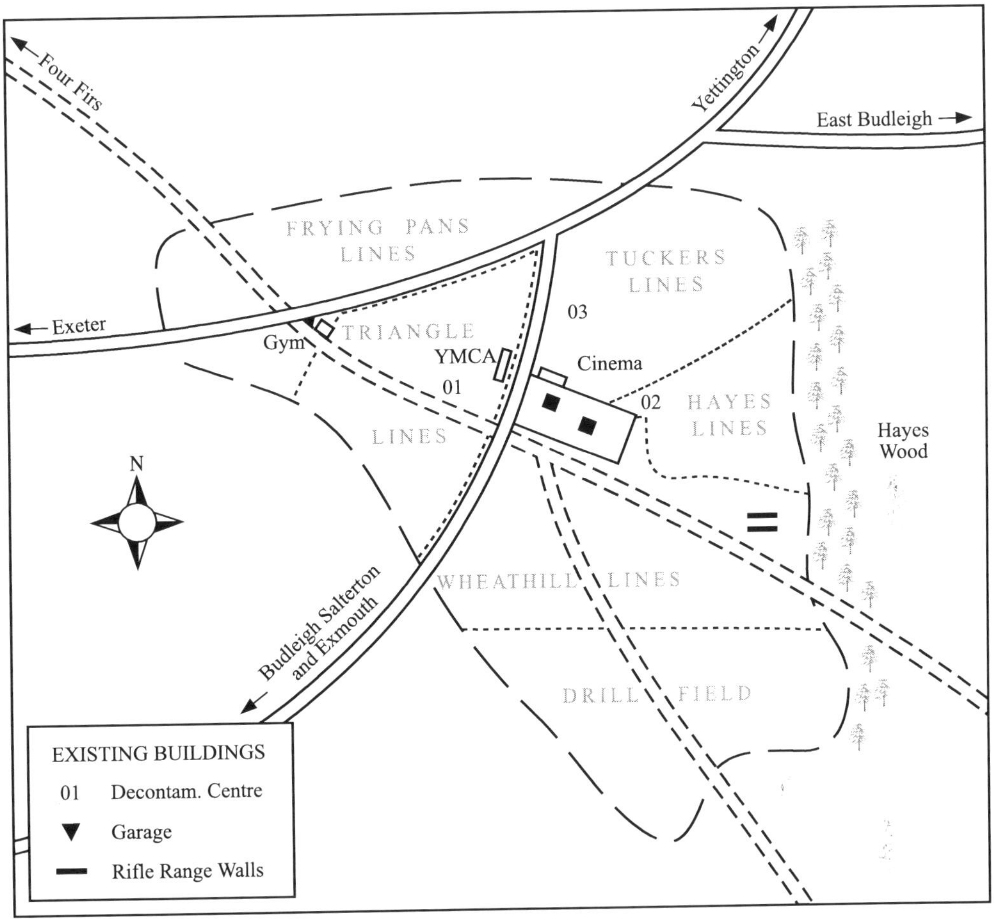

Map of Dalditch Camp

At the time building started on this vast project, the 7th and 8th RM Battalions of 103 RM Brigade were forming up again after their disintegration at Exton the previous January: and 648 men were living under canvas (mostly on the Wheathill site) with their Commandant, Captain A D B Godfrey. Accommodation for 5,000 men was being planned, to be housed in 378 twelve-man Nissen Huts, each thirty-six feet square, with a further 107 huts for office, stores, workshops. drying rooms and medical use; each sub-area to be fully self-contained with a share of all the basic facilities. Wheathill was the first site to be completed and by the end of that November of 1941 there were 2,100 of all ranks housed within it.

Plumbing and Sewerage

Ask any former Dalditch man what he remembers about the place and he will invariably answer 'Oil Lamps (pre-electric light installation), rats and "The Dog"'. The latter does not allude to the four-legged variety but the well known intestinal disorder, and since the facts have been revealed one can only wonder why the entire population of Budleigh Salterton was not wiped out by an epidemic resulting from this camp's insanitary conditions at the off-set! Small householders, frustrated by local council planning restrictions, can take heart from the fact that 'even the mighty can tumble', as in this instance when the Ministry of Health for Exmouth and East Budleigh was not consulted when plans were drawn up for the camp. As the men from the ministry discovered what was going on they respectfully pointed out to the War Office that the site covered long established watersheds supplying their area and 'Could they please move on!' By this time it was a bit late as galleys and latrines had already been erected adjacent to drains, and 'Their Lordships' were not prepared to dally much longer (Didn't the Ministry of Health realise there was a war on?), so a compromise was made whereby the huts were resited some distance away from these amenities. The problem did not end there however, but without elaborating into lurid details of the sewage disposal twixt latrine Elsan bucket and the four 9000 gallon tanks in lower Hayes section, it was soon discovered that through a defect causing overflowing at this source, 'effluence' was running via drains into the Hayes Barton stream and thence into Budleigh Salterton's water supply!

It is noted that a 'Professor of Applied Hygiene' visited the camp on 27 July 1942, so perhaps we can assume that between then and the November following, when Ministry of Health Inspectors arrived to check the new filter beds in Hayes Woods, Dalditch had got it's plumbing in order!

Each of the sub-areas had two dining halls and galleys of 250 man capacity, with a Senior Non-comissioned Officers' Mess attached to one galley, but only four had Officers' Messes (with galleys) as the one at Wheathill was double the size to cover Hayes Lines also. Wheathill, being the main centre, contained the only cinema, which opened on 3 Aug 1942 with the film *49th Parallel*, made the previous year and starring Robert Beatty, Leslie Howard, Glynis Johns, James Mason, Anton Walbrook, Eric Portman and Laurence Olivier. It also had the central Post Office from which sub-area 'posties' carried out a two way traffic, the telephone exchange, and the electric power transformer supplied from the East Budleigh grid... as well as the largest parade ground. Frying Pans had a gymnasium that doubled as a church (as did the cinema) whilst Triangle and Hayes boasted Naafi buildings; there were recreation huts in each section.

Dalditch turned to a number of sources for its supplies, of which a 28-day emergency ration was supposed to exist; vegetables by local purchase, bread from an Exmouth bakery, meat from Exeter, and the bulk of dry stores from Plymouth's Victualling Yard. Water in the initial stages came by road in tankers from Exton Camp until it could be piped from nearby Squabmoor Reservoir and stored in 20,000 gallon tanks at Wheathill and Frying Pans.

On 21 January 1942 the advance party of 10 RM Battalion arrived to take over Tuckers Lines, and the remainder filed in on 30 January to a strength of 660 of all ranks; they were closely followed by three officers and 147 other ranks of 'Q' Company RM Engineers on 9 February plus a rear party of twenty-four the next day. 4/5 May saw the influx of 31st Light Battery RM (formerly the 31st RM Howitzer Battery) having already served in Norway, Calais and at the Combined Operations Centre Inverary... they might well have added Dakar to the list but for the fact the officer leading this ill-fated expedition (Operation Menace, August 1940) noticed one man drop his rifle on 'Present Arms' and mistakenly assumed that they were not sufficiently trained to be included in his venture! The 32nd Light Battery RM joined them soon afterwards from the Orkneys, but from thence onwards they seem to have got involved with a mixture of other units and drifted on their way six months later, collecting 130 recruits from Exton on the way.

Another group of nomads were the North Irish Horse, a Territorial unit who drifted in groups between 6/10 May to a total of eleven officers and 149 ranks (plus tanks in lieu of horses)... but the situation obviously didn't suit them as they moved on elsewhere just fifteen days later!

For reasons best known to themselves 20 (Training) RM Battalion of 104 (Training) RM Brigade had moved out of Sunshine (Holiday!) Camp, Hayling Island that January setting up a new Headquarters at Langbrook on the Langstone Road leading into Havant on 11 March whilst deploying many of the men on Stobs Castle Exercise. Other units of Brigader A N William's Brigade, 15 (Machine Gun) and 18 RM Battalion were meanwhile occupied at Pennally and Saudersfoot (South Wales) when word reached him about Dalditch, so a 'recce party' was sent down on 15 March and Headquarters advance party swooped down to Exmouth on 3 April, with the main party following five days later, to set up business in the Palm Court Hotel (additional accommodation at 'Harbour View') and like the cuckoo sat casting envious glances at the 'very desirable Dalditch nest' as somewhere to bring all their chicks into one roost!

Surprisingly during all this upheaval they had managed to pass out their first intake of trainees in April, and then mysteriously Headquarters issued an order on 14 May instructing all the Brigade to undertake a standard swimming test of thirty yards in Battle Dress and equipment; were they planning to infiltrate Dalditch by swimming across the reservoir I wonder?

Lieutenant Colonel F B Pym, Commanding 20 (Training) RM Battalion arrived in Exmouth from Hayling Island with Major G P Pease on 6 June and during the next few days discussions took place with the Brigadier and staff of 103 RM Brigade already in residence , resulting in a complete 'take-over bid'. Administrative control then passed from 103 to 104 (Training) Brigade on 17 June and the very next day an advance party of 20 (Training) Battalion moved in to Tucker's Lines (the main party on 8 July) followed by 15 RM Battalion from Wales the day after (their main party on 3 July). Major G Underhill OBE DSC joined 'Camp Staff Dalditch' on 26 June and assumed the Commandant's duties from Captain Godfrey who became Barrack-master, with the rank of Major.

Lympstone Grange

On 16 July Brigade HQ moved out of the Palm Court Hotel and into Lympstone Grange at the top of Strawberry Hill road, leading from that village, and where new bungalows have recently been built to the right of this house, some Nissen Huts were erected at some stage after the commandeering, to accommodate Headquarters staff.

The only other point of interest that month was 'Exercise Howitzer' that took place 25–28 July in which 20 (Training) Battalion took part. One had to imagine the whole of Cornwall plus that part of Devon west of a line between Barnstaple and Teignmouth as an island captured by two battalions of Japanese, concentrated around Plymouth and the 'capital', Tavistock. Fortunately for the citizens of Plymouth, 102 RM Brigade met with complete success following a surprise dawn raid putting the 'enemy' to rout, but the same cannot be said for 101 Brigade assault in the Tavistock area.

101 RM Brigade moved out of Dalditch shortly after this 'Paper Battle' to make way for Mobile Naval Base Defence Organisation 2 (Engineer Company) who chose now to move in.

Now 20 (Training) Battalion and 21 (Holding) Battalion amalgamated on 20 October to form the RM Infantry Training Centre, undertaking Phase Two of the training syllabus as a follow-up for recruits passing out from Exton on completion of Phase One, and likewise later on Continuous Service Squads came from Deal when the Depot opened for business again, following the run-down in 1940 due to bombing.

104 (Training) RM Brigade then began looking for other straws to clutch, and on 12 November a new unit, 22 (Training) RM Battalion, formed with Major D A C Shephard as Officer Commanding, Captain J M Buckett (Adjutant) and Major D D Stewart as Second in Command… their purpose 'To be a Young Soldier's Battalion for the holding and training of Marines under nineteen years of age'. They occupied Frying Pan's Lines on 23 November and brought out their first Daily Orders that same day, then started the first Cadre Course on 25 November to train suitable Junior Non-Commissioned Officers for instructional duties as the first 218 'young trained soldiers' arrived next day from the Infantry Training Centre Royal Marines. 'A' Company came under the watchful eye of Sergeant Gilden and 'B' Company had Sergeant Shepherd (not to be confused with the Commanding Officer!) backed up by Sergeant Fish with drill and discipline in the hands of QMSI A Webb and Field Training under Lieutenant W H Ollis. In addition to evening instructions from 1730 every Monday, Tuesday and Thursday they had to carry out at least one night exercise per week, and with the directive from the Commanding Officer to instructors, 'It will be appreciated that only the highest standards can be accepted'. I imagine everyone in that unit was kept well on their toes!

Training course

Settling Down

We now progress through into 1943 as Major Shephard became Acting Lieutenant Colonel in the New Year, Lieutenant (Quartermaster) Norman Finch VC (of Zeebrugge fame) joined 22 (Training) RM Battalion on 25 February, and another celebrity, pianist/composer Vivian Ellis (*Bless the Bride* and many other musicals) as a Lieutenant

RNVR moved into Headquarters on 8 March (his association with the Corps also included a period at Stonehouse Barracks) and two days later Lieutenant Colonel B J D Lumsden visited Dalditch to lecture on 'Hints for Budding Escapists'… I have heard that conditions there were pretty bad but until now I hadn't realised the situation was quite so desparate!

In the New Year also Lympstone Grange changed from being Brigade Headquarters to Headquarters Royal Marines Training Group (Devon) and Brigadier A C St Clair-Morford arrived on 25 January to relieve Brigadier H T Newman in office.

By April the Infantry Training Centre Royal Marines had doubled its intake of recruits and at the same time ranks completing this course were being drafted to the new set-up at Towyn (Royal Marine Training Group Wales – see *The Globe and Laurel*, February 1976). An interesting entry in the 'Top Secret Signals' at this time was the arrival of sixty-six Royal Navy commandos in the last week of October, staying only one week then moving on to Plymouth.

Having visited Dalditch myself in all seasons, viewing it through swirling mist, incessant rain and brilliant sunshine, I can understand how its varying moods influenced men's opinions of it… mud featured in many of the *Globe and Laurel* reports issued from this quarter, but by April 1944 the journal was able to state that all tracks had been gravelled and main roads tarmaced and signposted (Church Lane and Wheathill Road etc). Major Alastair Donald, the Corps Historical Records Officer, recalls the pleasant tasks he undertook as a recruit in 1943, engaged in collecting rubble from bombed sites in Exeter and how to ease their load on the return trip, he sat tossing lumps of rock from the back of the truck to ensure a speedy conclusion of this fatigue duty on their return to Dalditch where the rubble was used to lay road foundations.

On one such engagement, after nonchalantly heaving one chunk of concrete over a roadside hedge, an irate courting couple jumped up and hurled abuse at the quickly disappearing truck!

Whether 20 (Training) Battalion brought its 'Sunshine Band' in the move from Hayling Island to Dalditch I cannot say, but not to be outdone, 22 (Training) Battalion formed its own 'Marineers Dance Band' during this period, destined for fame (and fortune?) throughout the surrounding district; at about the same time an RN School of Music Band was attached to the Infantry Training Centre Royal Marines, sharing themselves amongst 22 and 23 Battalions as well as Camp Staff and Holding Company… but I have no indication as to whether the two bands were connected in any way. Dalditch was also now well established on the ENSA Circuit and like Exton was producing much of its own talent, which attracted audiences from the nearby American Base as well as entertaining their own mates.

By June 1944 the Infantry Training Centre Royal Marines were football League Champions, and at Whit weekend the unit held a big public sports day at Exmouth's

Cricket Ground, with the Band in attendance, proving so popular that the experience was repeated the following August Bank Holiday! Between these twin events Dalditch suffered three losses as 22 (Training) Battalion moved to Towyn, closely followed by 23 Battalion with whom it shortly merged… and 'Sally' the camp's canine mascot sadly died after three years duty!

Brigadier R H Campbell CB MC ADC came in May to open a YMCA in Triangle Lines which proved very popular, and shortly beforehand also opened a .22 rifle range; then about the same time the khaki-clad trainees there witnessed an event which filled them with awe and envy… this strange phenomenon being a ship's detachment marching into camp dressed in Blues!

I can't say when the 'School of Mines' (formerly RM Siege Regiment), crept in from Dover, but their going was noted on 14 November 1944, bound for the Royal Marine Training Group (Wales). Through the winter and spring of 1945 the 'production line' continued turning out young eager men whilst the Allied troops, including many trained here, battled their way through Europe and the Far East, drawing the War to a close. Amongst the many originating at Dalditch were the 8th Battalion (now 41 Commando RM), 9th Battalion (46 Commando RM) and 7th Battalion (48 Commando RM); then on 24 August 1944, 27 RM Battalion formed up here under Lieutenant Colonel P W O H Phibbs (replaced by Lieutenant Colonel N H Tailyour in January, by which time they had moved up to Gailes Camp near Irvine in Scotland) and 30 RM Battalion (Lieutenant Colonel T K Walker) formed up here in January to team up later with 28 Battalion (Lieutenant Colonel J A Taplin) as 116 RM Infantry Brigade, serving in Holland and Germany under Brigadier S G B Paine OBE.

In the latter stages of the War, a number of Prisoners of War were exchanged with the Germans on the understanding that they would not serve in operational theatres of the war. Eighty-eight Royal Marines went to Dalditch via Exton during August 1943, repatriated from Stalag VIII B having been taken prisoner at Crete.

A month after VE Day the 'veterans' were released to 'civvy street', and the first three from Dalditch were Lieutenant Finch VC (who transferred from 22 RM Battalion to Camp Staff in October 1943), CSM Parnham and Sergeant Goodman; Lieutenant Colonel Wooley handed over command of the camp to Lieutenant Colonel J C Westall and Major General A N Williams OBE returned from the Royal Marine Training Group (Wales) to relieve Brigadier A H E Reading of the Royal Marine Training Group (Devon) Lympstone Grange. From there Marine George Bowman went through the demob process and then returned to do precisely the same job as gardener in plain clothes… but the continuity could not last. By May of the next year Headquarters Staff had to vacate the country house in favour of 'Belsen Grange' (as they termed Dalditch!).

The Decline and Fall

At the camp the surrounding barbed wire entanglements had been removed by October 1945, as 60 Reinforcement Holding Unit moved in and Motor Transport Driving and Signals Schools followed in March next year; then the Military Instructors' Department prepared to move to the Infantry School at Bickleigh, Holding Battalion ceased to function and all other departments started running down... rumours abounded over the future of Dalditch! An Educational Vocational Training Centre moved in from Ivybridge at the end of 1945, but the two Captains, T H Jones and G Yeomans with their staff of four Corporals and four Marines hardly had time to settle before being packed off to Plymouth in August.

By September 'Camp Staff', who had transferred from Triangle to Tucker's Lines, now closed down whilst the Motor Transport School found better accommodation at Alsager (near Crewe) and Signals School moved on also. With the once packed camp now looking decidedly forlorn, with only the Infantry Training Centre Royal Marines and Headquarters in residence, it is perhaps ironic that in its demise, Dalditch retched the peak of its achievements on the sporting field as 'Tunney Cup' football champions (beating Plymouth 5–0), winners of the 'Mead Cup' and their marksmen carried off most of the trophies (ten in fact) at the Browndown Small Arms Contest! It is believed that 450 Continuous Service Squad, coming from Deal, was the last to carry out Phase Two of training with the Infantry Training Centre Royal Marines at Dalditch.

Isolated and insanitary it might have been, but Dalditch surprisingly had its loyal subjects who sung its praises and earnestly hoped that their 'home' would survive when the final choice was made on which of the two camps to keep open... but it really stood no chance for a number of reasons, not least of which was Exton's superior accommodation. With almost indecent haste, workmen began dismantling the huts as they emptied, and whilst all records of Exmouth ranks were despatched to Plymouth Headquarters, a fleet of trucks loaded up men and equipment for the transfer to the new Infantry Training Centre Royal Marines Lympstone (Exton having by now virtually disappeared in favour of the new name)... yet even here as they prepared to take on Phase One and Two training the future was not certain, after all Towyn and newly acquired Bickleigh vied for importance, and no doubt all but the 'Top Brass' watched and waited to see the outcome. I wonder if anyone then envisaged the transformation that would overtake Lympstone during the next four decades?

But for Dalditch the fight was now over, although this heartland that through the centuries felt the tread of invading Roman, Saxon and Danish armies, and civil war 'Royalists' and 'Parliamentarians' campaigning hereabouts, has not yet borne the last Royal Marine boot whilst the Commando Training Centre Royal Marines continue training upon it. Here, where Sir Walter Raleigh played during his childhood at nearby Hayes Barton Farm, and today's recruits amble nonchalantly past on map reading exercises without perhaps a thought to what hallowed ground they tread, nature reclaims its wilderness. 'Dalditch Camp is no more', *The Globe and Laurel* dramatically declared at the end of 1946.

The outdoor life

Part Three

RM Infantry/Commando Training Centre

Lymptone

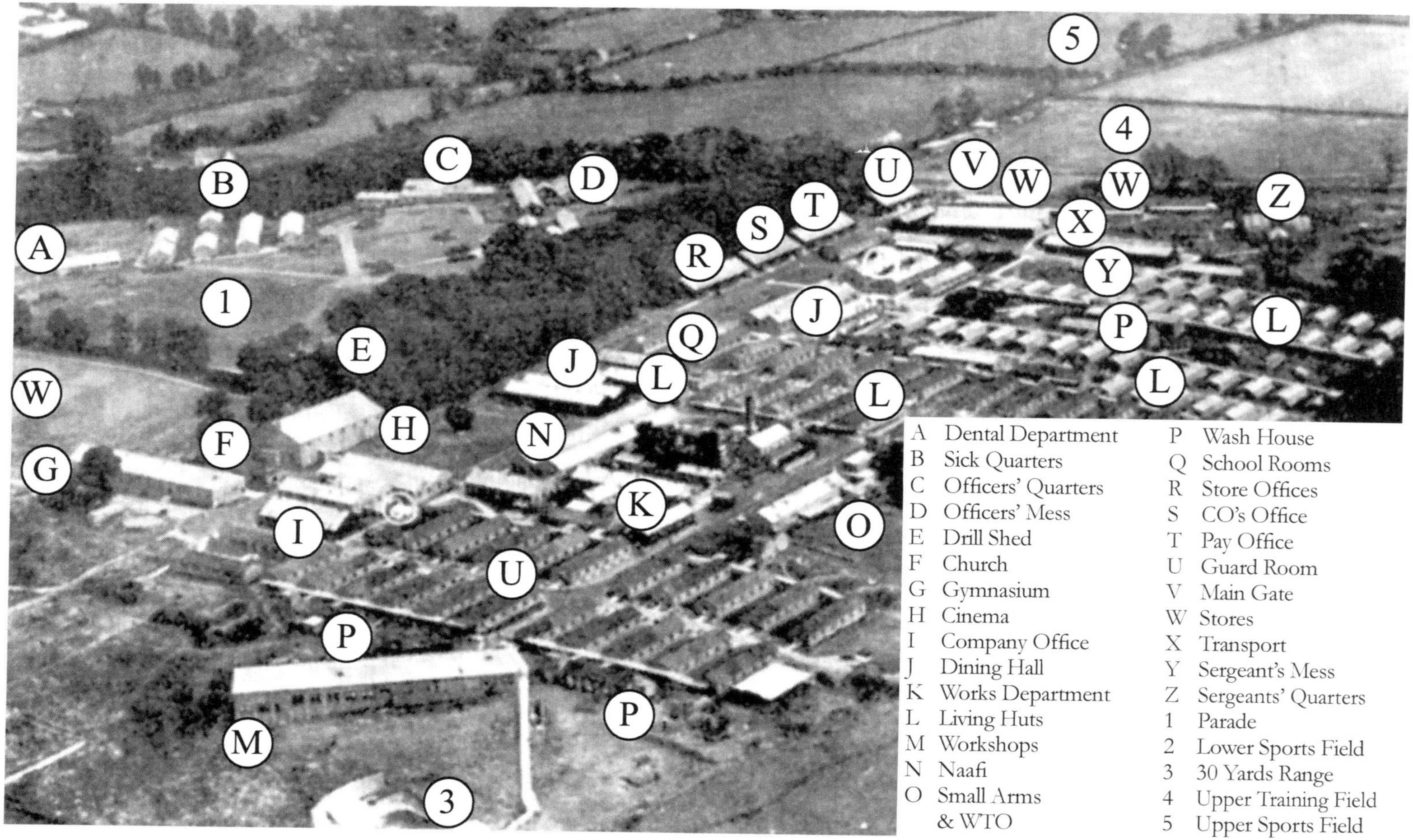

View of Lympstone Camp

RM Infantry/Commando Training Centre – Lympstone

RM Depot Exton officially became RM Depot Lympstone on 5 September 1941, although the first *Globe and Laurel* reference to the new name came with the February 1944 edition and war diaries mention it as early as May two years previously, yet the camp continued its dual nomenclature for at least another year, whilst in one edition of the Corps Journal we find three separate contributors referring to the same place as 'Depot (D)', 'Exton' and 'Lympstone'... but certainly well before the war's end, 'Exton' had been dropped by all except the locals and its early inmates who continued to cherish the title as one boasts of membership to some exclusive club!

In Part One I left you mid 1942 with a completed camp just as its near neighbour Dalditch was rising out of the heartland, and according to a letter sent by Brigadier N K Jolly to the Adjutant General, Devon Council had widened the road in front of the Depot, laid a pathway from Woodbury Road Station (Exton), and the camp had taken on a very pleasing appearance, This letter also inferred that the field opposite the main gate was again 'tented' in March 1941, this time to accommodate the 1st Engineering Company RM.

Corporal A P Thompson was now firmly installed as Warden of the 500 yards Straight Point Range, after faithfully reporting Lympstone's first two years of 'growing pains' in the Corps Journal, whilst other firing ranges in use locally by the trainees during this period were at Starcross, Merrivale and Scorrington. By the time Lympstone established its own thirty yard range in May 1944, Pat Thompson was back there again sending in his despatches once more, informing us that the RM tradesmen who constructed it, using materials from blitzed sites in Exmouth, at the same time built a mini-steeple and a vestry for the camp church.

And the Raids Came

On most evenings throughout 1941–42 the drone of enemy aircraft could be heard surging inland to bomb other cities, but although Exmouth received a few incendiary bombs on its outskirts earlier, it was on 18 January 1941 that this town took its first major battering in the densely built-up area bounded by Chapel, Church and Rolle Streets, and this flattened site remained vacant until 1978 when under a redevelopment scheme, the Royal Marines Association Branch unfortunately lost their Gibraltar

Club premises that stood on the fringe. Later on in 1942 and into the next year, the Luftwaffe changed their tactics and went in for daylight 'hit and run' raids, often using just a single aircraft, but then eight came in on the final raid of 26 February 1943 when the worst casualties occurred, and by the last 'all clear' the sirens had sounded 469 times.

Many troops were employed in rescue and clearance work within the district, including 'Royals', and I doubt if anyone from 10 RM Battalion serving at Dalditch will forget the night of 25–26 April 1942 when, having carried out this debris clearing only the week before, they were now engaged as 'Nazi Parachutists' for 'Exercise Raleigh' into which Army and Home Guard units were also drawn; their purpose to create confusion on the road to Exeter during a pretended bombing raid... well, the 'confusion' developed alright, as they got caught up in a real raid!

On the training side, recruit squads passed with regularity to Dalditch for Phase Two of their 'upbringing', occasionally interspersed with 'special guests' such as the RAF Non-Commissioned Officers' classes commencing in February 1943 in five groups of half a dozen at a time. Since these forerunners of the RAF Regiment set off from here we have now come full circle in having at least one member of that force back on the training staff. During the war the two local RAF stations were at Beer and Branscombe, and there was also the Exeter Airport site of course.

The Phase One syllabus was increased from six to eight weeks with EX 583 squad in May 1943, whilst Phase Two training at the Royal Marines Infantry Training Centre, Dalditch, which originally stood at only eight weeks had risen to fourteen weeks by November 1945, sixteen the following January, and seventeen by the end of that year when Dalditch closed and the Royal Marines Infantry Training Centre moved into Lympstone.

For the benefit of the uninitiated, Phase One included kitting-up, lectures (including Corps history), physical training, drill, bayonet fighting, basic small arms and Bren Gun drills... and the receiving of gratuitous issues of jabs! With the assault course, advanced weapon training, range work, night firing and field craft (involving cooking and survival) coming into Phase Two, the last week of which was usually spent under canvas near Ottery St Mary during the latter stages of the Dalditch era at least.

The Elusive Provost (RM Police)

Their *Globe and Laurel* reports gave nothing away except a vague location somewhere in the Exmouth area (it was in sporting fixtures that units invariably gave some clues to vicinities!) and mentioned only Clarks Hill for the motorcycle training ground... the fact that nobody I interviewed in the area had ever heard of the place nor could it be found on the Ordnance Survey Map only serves to illustrate just how elusive this branch was!

A subsequent clue to the location of Clarks Hill and the Provost HQ was revealed by Lieutenant Colonel F F Clark RM, who gave this report:

> "I was appointed Deputy Provost Marshal RM on 26 October 1944 and had my headquarters at the Imperial Hotel in Exmouth until 25 February 1946 when the RM Provost Depot then closed. The Imperial and two private hotels on The Beacon accommodated staff and trainee Provost. The Officers' Mess was a corner house not far from the Imperial, whilst stores etc were kept in two terraced houses about a quarter mile away. Some of the motor cycle training was carried out on Black Hill, Lympstone Common (which is on the map and no doubt renamed by the men after their Commanding Officer!), where additional hazards 'The Snake' and 'The Camel' etc, were constructed.
>
> "When I arrived at Exmouth the unit was commanded by Major Frank Little who later took a Provost Unit to the Far East. Trained Provost were drafted to RM Units in the UK and Europe, and there was a London Unit of approximately sixty housed in Chelsea Barracks.
>
> "The Exmouth Provost Depot had close contacts with the US Naval Police and Devon Police. We were called out to assist the latter on an incident which nearly became the 'Battle of Okehampton'. Due to trouble at a local dance hall between a Polish Unit and a British Army Unit, both sides had raided their respective guard-rooms and were advancing into town with rifles and ball Ammunition. An RM Provost Unit (and men of 28 RM Battalion) also armed with rifles, was hurried from Exmouth, but luckily both groups were diverted."

Another nearby hotel, up on the hill (The Beacon) was also a dormitory for the men, while one garage in town was converted into a Mess Hall and a second one used for storage of vehicles and motor cycles. When 35 RM Provost formed up in the latter stages of the war for Far East service, the house of Lady Byron, also on The Beacon (next to that of Lady Nelson) also provided accommodation. Earlier, about thirty men of RM Training Group Devon Provost Company were at Lympstone Grange and became RM Division Provost Company on 1 Nov 1943 before moving into Exmouth Headquarters.

The RM Provost wore the distinctive 'Red Cap' cover over khaki or blue caps, and other than the corps badge looked identical to their Army equivalents who taught the original instructors all the tricks of their trade at the Corps of Military Police, Mytchett Depot near Aldershot.

Other than lurking around the local pubs at closing time to harass poor unsuspecting Bootnecks enjoying a quiet evening out, these men did much useful work in security and convoy control etc, both at home and abroad!

C J Mahoney, who had a short period in both London and Naples as the Naval Provost Marshal, testified to the excellent work discharged by the Royal Marine 'Redcaps'; policing in Naples and running the Naval Courts for merchant seamen was no sinecure. He recalls that the main body of the Provost were in Exmouth's Imperial Hotel by the late summer of 1945, and all basic training was done there and in the nearby countryside. Lieutenant Colonel F H Nicholson, a distinguished First Drill in pre-war days, and King's Badgeman, was Naval Provost Marshal for North West Europe.

An RM Provost

By November 1945 Chatham RM Provost Detachment had closed down, Portsmouth and Plymouth followed likewise a month later, London, Royal Marine Training Group Wales and MT School Detachments disappeared by the following March leaving only Headquarters Royal Marine Training Group Devon operational within the UK. Number 3 RM Provost were meanwhile heavily committed in occupied Europe whilst 35 RM Provost, with Headquarters in Ceylon (Colombo) spread themselves around the far eastern theatre of war in such places as Bombay, Rangoon, Tokyo, Hong Kong and Singapore; and from this latter detachment Corporals Isaacs and O'Reilly, as bodyguards for the Commander-in-Chief, were amongst the first to reach and relieve the notorious Changi Prisoner of War camp .

Remnants of the Headquarters Provost moved out of Exmouth to Dalditch Camp in February 1946, and then in June the last Red Cap cover went into mothballs as those not due for demobilization were split up into other units. Thus, when the overseas representatives returned the following year and dispersed, the 'Corps' own 'Military Police' ceased to function in that specific form, the disciplinary duties then being undertaken by each unit's temporary 'Regimental Police' until a new branch with MP 1 qualifications was introduced in the 1960s, again receiving a guiding hand from their Army cousins of the Royal Military Police now at the Chichester Depot.

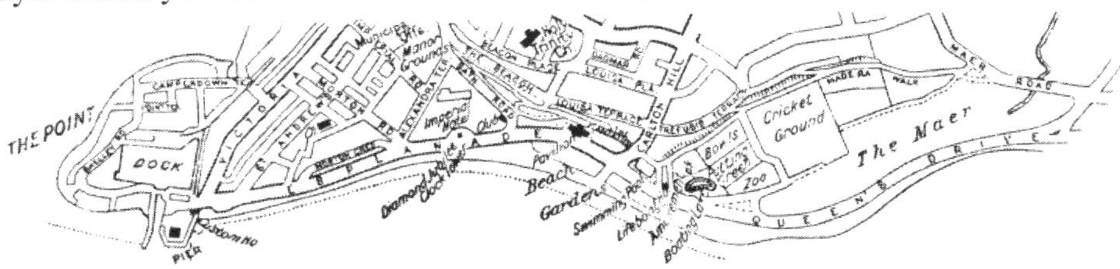

The Exmouth Coast

The Social Scene

Many buildings in Exmouth were commandeered by HM Forces during the war, particularly hotels, and other than the two mentioned in Part Two (The Palm Court, now renamed Seacrest House as private flats: and Harbour View Cafe – both on the seafront) the most notable was the Imperial, then privately owned, which housed RN and RM personnel and was then considerably larger than at present, one wing having been destroyed by fire in 1974.

In addition there were one or two servicemen's canteens, and rather late in the day NAAFI opened a branch in January 1946 which has since closed. Royal Marines did not have the monopoly of this town then, as they do now, for whilst the Navy and RAF presence was felt in perhaps small doses, there was a very considerable Army contingent of British, American and Polish troops.

Imperial Hotel (pre-fire)

For a short period after the war, as the Grange was vacated, Lower Nutwell Farmhouse, adjacent to the camp, was taken on as the Commandant's quarters, but is now back in private use again.

Social life within the camp went on much as usual throughout the remaining war years, with the weekly band concerts sometimes augmented by the RM Infantry Training Centre band, fortnightly dances in addition to the film and occasional ENSA shows, boxing matches and other sporting events (by 1946 there were four Royal Marines from Lympstone in the Exeter City Football Club). The fourth annual Depot Horticultural Show reached a new peak in 1944 when 750 visitors on 19 August raised seventy pounds ten shillings towards the Exton Prisoner of War Fund, which in less than a year had realised £1,300 for the despatch of 'food and comforts' parcels to ex-Lympstone men held in Prisoner of War camps by the enemy. Lieutenant Colonel F W Dewhurst, on his second tour of duty here as Commanding Officer, officiated at the prize giving inside the theatre whilst outside Warrant Officer W Smith entertained those taking tea on the lawn with his twenty-five piece band, and the side-shows continued to rake in the pennies! It was a small crowd however compared to the 3,082 who were later to flood through the gates for the first official open day to the general public on 24 September 1947 (*The Globe and Laurel*, November 1947: pages 260–263).

In August 1944 our old friend Corporal Thompson wrote his 'farewell' message in *The Global and Laurel* when departing for Plymouth, where at Stonehouse Barracks he was a very popular man, next year raising the Demob Chits until suddenly he found his own before him, which he duly signed himself, leaving the Corps finally on 12 September 1945 after a total of twenty-seven years service, to settle in his Bristol home city where in 1986 he attained his eighty-eighth year! At the beginning of the year Lieutenant Colonel F W Dewhurst also left, handing over to Lieutenant Colonel S G B Paine OBE, coming from 116 RM Infantry Brigade, who in turn was to hand over to Lieutenant Colonel R W Sankey DSO DSC only six months later.

One Door Closes, Another Opens

On 18 August 1946 the Pre-OCTU (preparatory course for young officer candidates) closed its doors at Lympstone with Hostilities Only 44 Course, whilst the Depot had taken on a new role the previous spring with the training of RM Engineer recruit entries.

The biggest change however was to come at the end of 1946 with the closure of Dalditch and subsequent transfer of RM Infantry Training to RM Depot Lympstone, under it's new title ITCRM (as distinct from RMITC at Dalditch).

It was a most emotional and chaotic time for the camp as old friends were taking their leave, including the WRNS unit, and a continual convoy of road transport milled around between the two camps transferring 'lock, stock and barrel' all the necessary equipment and furnishings for the new set-up… and, rather appropriately I feel, amidst all this feverish activity the Dramatic Society chose to perform Noel Coward's play Hay Fever in the camp theatre! Down at the WRNS quarters Chief Petty Officer Ferguson BEM, whom you may recall in Part One came here as a Leading Wren in charge of twenty young ladies in September 1941, was throwing a farewell party prior to withdrawing with 'her girls' as dramatically as they had arrived, leaving a vacancy that was not filled until 28 August 1974 when 'Marens' moved into newly built accommodation.

1 November 1946 was the date set for the official change-over of Lympstone's new role and title, by which time the last of the six remaining recruit squads had completed Phase One training (this part then became exclusive to Depot Deal for both Continuous Service and National Service lads) and they then concentrated on Phase Two syllabus only. Headquarters RM Infantry Training Group Devon was now closed down, and personnel records and control of Infantry Training Centre Royal Marines (ITCRM) passed to the command of Plymouth Group.

An 'inventory Check' at the time revealed 3,000 officers and men living in seventy-four huts enclosed in an area of fifty-four acres within a boundary of one and a quarter miles! Broken down this represented sixty officers, thirteen Companies of three platoons each, plus a complete Infantry Battalion with a total of eighty-two vehicles of varying types to convey them around! Lympstone was now very much alive and well with between 1,000 and 1,500 recruits under training at any given time, and on completion of which some went on to Bickleigh Infantry School for specialisation or to the Commando Training Centre at Towyn (North Wales) which, for a short time had taken over this role from Achnacarry before it too closed down, and Plymouth took temporary control.

From its humble beginnings seven years earlier Lympstone had, to all intents and purposes, progressed to 'near perfection', with two small churches now, a Corps Military Library built up to 1,200 books for recruit study, and many other facilities… yet 'Their Lordships' were still not satisfied and many changes were to come, so that by the year of 1986 we now have an entirely rebuilt camp, beyond all recognition to any who first served there.

Changing Roles and Development

Early in 1951 the Officer Training Wing moved in from Bickleigh Infantry School, just six men in the first intake, two of whom were Corps Commission candidates and parachutists, to be joined later by further batches totalling a complement of forty. The Officers Mess also acquired some material additions at this time, as a piano, table-centre, two paintings, some silver and other items of furniture arrived from Chatham Barracks which was closing down.

There were two intakes of boys between the ages of sixteen and seventeen in August and October 1958: who were known as Youth Entries One and Two (YEI and YE2) but were later amalgamated to form Junior Entry Squad Number One (JE1). The charge of these young men for their first year of training was given to Lieutenant Thomas Seccombe RM. They spent a year at Deal before being split up, so that eighteen of the eldest boys went to Lympstone for Commando training, while the others remained at Deal for further training.

With the temporary closure of Stonehouse Barracks (Plymouth) for a 'care and maintenance' period, the Senior Non-Commissioned Officers' Training Wing and Specialised Training moved to Lympstone in February 1960, followed by the Commando Specialist Training in April, which included Heavy Weapons, Cliff Assault, and Assault Engineers. These bodies joined up with the resident 'X' Troop to form a new Commando Training Wing centred around the old 'C' Company Lines.

Previously there had been four recruit companies, A, B, C and D; of these only A and C survived, with the former as the National Service Company, but to make way for the new units these now amalgamated into a single Recruit Training Wing in February.

The last of the National Service recruits were in 939 Squad, finishing their Phase Two training here early in 1961, and thus were due for release two years later, just as Lympstone started to undergo its facelift.

In the autumn of 1959 the Sergeant's Mess had some alterations and foundations were laid for an extension which increased recreational facilities, but under the redevelopment plans, drawn up in five stages to cover an estimated twelve years' period, the first actual replacements were the Drill Shed in 1960 and the wooden huts of the Officers' Mess, the latter taking about a year for completion, in bricks and mortar.

Lieutenant General M C Cartwright-Taylor opened the first of the new recruit accommodation blocks on 12 July 1963, by which time four others were also erected, awaiting completion, and already 'a blot on the rural skyline' according to the *Western Morning News* of 29 June. Some locals obviously viewed the new 'skyscrapers' with alarm, and the Earl of Devon, residing opposite in Powderham Castle, who no doubt had the most cause for complaint, suggested the planting of trees around the camp to hide it! Although trees do adorn the site, even now the white buildings stand out clearly from Exmouth and the western river shoreline.

The site selected for the new barrack blocks was at the top of the slope above the old bayonet range. A total of seven new barrack blocks and four company offices were planned for this site, each of four storeys intended to accomodate 100 men, whilst the company office buildings were small, compact and single-storeyed. At Withycombe Raleigh thirty-six new married quarters for 'other ranks' were rising per schedule, with

The old and new Officers' Mess

the officer's quarters slowly progressing on the Admiralty land at Lympstone and War Office land at the Retreat in Topsham, but would not be ready for another two years.

By the end of 1966 the Mess and recreational block, including the Main Galley, Dining Halls, NAAFI and Junior Non-Commissioned Officers' Club was nearing completion; nearby were the NAAFI quarters and a trading centre designed to house the UIF-run amenities, Barber Shop, Pressing Shop, Laundry and Drying Room, a civilian Tailor's Shop... and the new automatic telephone exchange which came into operation that January. Also in progress were the practice rooms, stores and offices of the Plymouth Group Band and the seventh barrack block. Sports grounds were provided in the field opposite the main gate.

Exmouth Adoption Parade

Exmouth's adoption of the Corps took place on 11 May 1968 when a parade, depicting the various Royal Marine uniforms, wended its way through the town, whilst Exeter followed suit on 23 April 1977. Between these two events a new training syllabus had been introduced in Easter 1972 because of the popularity of the new initial short engagements. Divided into two phases, the purpose of Phase One (Commando Training) was preparation, covering the majority of individual skills and the physical build-up necessary for Phase Two, lasting fourteen weeks for adults and twenty-five weeks for juniors. This concentrated on team and group skills, all aspects of troop weapons and minor tactics up to section level, and included a week at the Amphibious Training Unit, Poole. The Infantry Training Centre RM changed to the Commando Training Centre RM on 24 August 1970.

By January 1976 the Junior Marines' Block and an extension to the Officers' Mess had been completed, work progressed on the new Sergeants' Mess and sadly the last tree holding the thirty foot ropes of the old assault course was felled! That Easter the Sergeants were at last able to take up residence in their new Mess, and since the New Year, recruits were now arriving here direct instead of via Depot Deal.

A unique event occurred on 3 May that year when the Mayor of Exeter joined the Commandant General and senior railway executives on an inaugural train service from Exeter scheduled to stop at the camp's very own station, Lympstone Commando, not only the first new station to be built in the western region this century, but the only one in the country designed exclusively for servicemen.

The old and new Sergeants' Mess (These opened on 14 May 1940 and 2 April 1974, respectively)

Lympstone Commando Station

Other special events included the first change-over of the Commando Group RM, outside of Whitehall on 11 April 1975, a rare visit by a Prime Minister (Harold Wilson) later that year; and the first member of the Royal Family to undertake the Commando Course (HRH Prince Charles) during November 1974. The younger Princes Andrew and Edward did likewise in 1980 and 1983 respectively, the latter actually joining the Corps on 5 September.

The fifth stage of modernisation was officially celebrated as completed with the unveiling of the 'Both Arms' Kenneth Armitage sculpture, in the newly named 'CGs Court' at the end of 1974, by which time the number of recruits' barrack blocks had been increased to nine, plus one of three storeys for trained ranks.

With 'D' Block (Salerno) being the first of the new four storied blocks to be opened on 12 July 1963, the last one was that for the Junior Entries Wing (Normandy), built to a completely different design and containing twenty barrack rooms, plus four 'quiet rooms', three television and two hobbies rooms, also Company and Troop offices. This block had the distinction of being officially opened at precisely 1158 hours on Monday 28 October 1974… exactly 310 years (to the minute) after the founding of the Corps.

Apart from the Corporals Block and one as yet unnamed ('F' Block), the remainder are known as Chosin, Dieppe, Kangaw, Limbang, Matapan, Montforterbeek, Normandy, Radfan, Salerno and Termoli.

Four years later the new £1.8 million physical and recreational training centre was completed; by which time the Physical Training Wing had moved in from Deal. A new church of St Alban was dedicated on 1 April 1981, in the presence of the

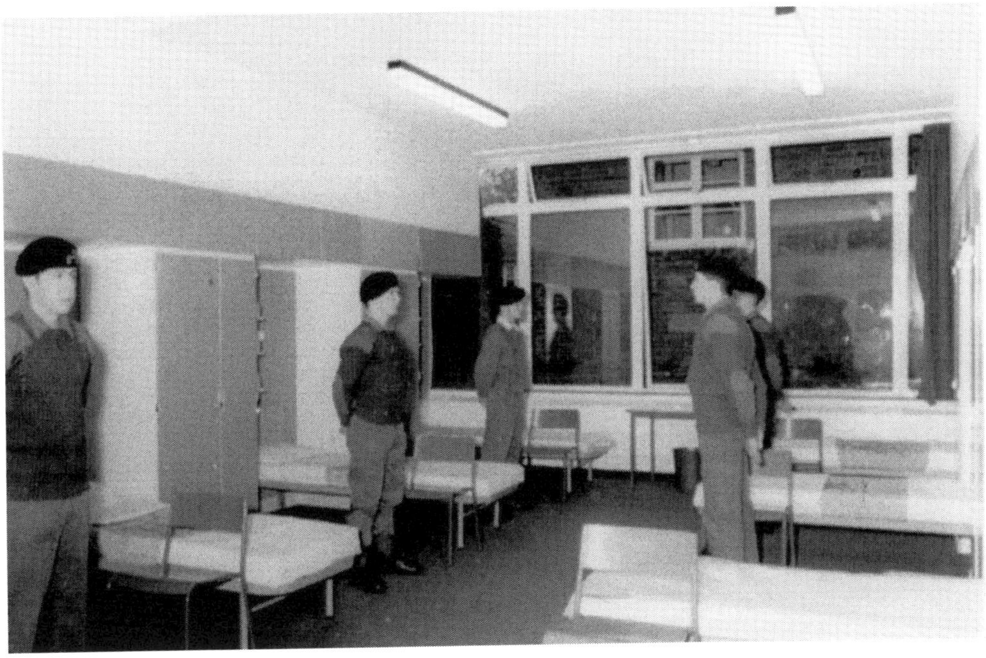

A new barrack room

Countess Mountbatten of Burma, and then when Major General Sir Jeremy Moore KCB OBE MC opened the new main presentation centre, Falklands Hall, on 6 May 1984 it could be said that Lympstone Camp's modernisation was complete. Only one of the original wooden huts now remains to remind any returning 'old boys' that this site is indeed that of the old Exton Camp, and one can only guess at their thoughts as they survey the vast complex of today! They might also compare the pay received by today's recruits, and envy their cars and seemingly marvellous conditions, but times (and prices) have dramatically changed since the formative days of the old Exton Camp, when the return bus fare from the main gate into Exmouth was just eight pence (three and a half pence in decimal coinage) or one shilling sixpence (seven and a half pence) to Exeter; by train it was six and a half pence (three pence) and one shilling one pence (five and a half pence) return respectively… and the fortnightly pay for a recruit was twenty-eight shillings (one pound and forty pence)!

Part Four

Personal Memories

Personal Memories

Marine C H Jones (PO/X 100327), who joined Royal Marine Reserve Depot Exton in 1940 as a conscript, made up his mind that he would not stay in the Corps after the war, and though not remembering much about the training, does recall there being no shore leave, and no hot water! There were approximately fifty men in his squad, under Colour Sergeant Peter's care, and after his six weeks at Exton he was drafted to the Naval Examination Service as a signaller, and served the war out as a member of the anti-contraband patrols in the Falmouth area. Marine M S J Burnett joined Exton in August 1941, when it was known as RM Training Group Devon (RMTG(D)), as a volunteer. It was a Thursday, he recalls, and kit having been drawn the following day they started their training on the parade square on Monday morning. Included in his training was Drill, weapon handling, physical training, assault course and first aid. 206 Squad also had fifty members, under the command of Colour Sergeant Smith, and at the end of his six weeks went on to Dalditch for a period of field firing, and thence on to the RM Beach Battalion. He enjoyed his training and would have signed on after the war if the pay had been better! Like Marine Jones, he never sampled the hot water supply!

Stan Marshall – Formerly EX 2738, Sergeant (Training)

'On 15 February 1940, a week before the first intake into Exton there was an intake into Eastney, of which I was one, comprising both volunteers and conscripts who completed their training there, prior to dispersing for specialist training for Mobile Naval Base Defence Organisation units.

'This intake was the last to have the EX prefix to their regimental numbers. The initial members of the Special Reserve had, originally, the prefix 'SR', which was later changed to EX, with three figure numbers, ours being four figures. The distinguishing feature of all these so-called Exton ranks was the fact that they were issued with Khaki Service Dress, Royal Marine pattern greatcoats and 1914–18 webbing. Both their uniforms were tailored to fit, after issue, and their greatcoats altered to the regulation fourteen inches from the deck. Most of us acquired forage caps – from Charlotte Street, I believe – for walking out, as we considered them to be smarter than what we called the 'side caps' with which we were issued.

'At the conclusion of basic training, we were given a week's leave, but unfortunately, on the very day of leave commencing, I was admitted to Haslar

Hospital with German Measles. On discharge, I returned to Eastney to find that the intake had returned from leave and been dispersed from their specialist training. There were few HOs (Hostilities Only) left in barracks, wearing KSD, the new intake having been issued with Battle Dress and Army Pattern Greatcoats.

'During our training we were in companies according to the identifying letter of our barrack block and the number of our room. Thus I was in 'K' Company, 58 Squad. Our instructor was Colour Sergeant 'Duff' Larker, whose name appeared amongst the Old Comrades not so long ago and our Rear Rank Instructor was Corporal 'Ginger' Fryer, who died tragically of Tuberculosis after the Norwegian Campaign. Our Company Sergeant Major was Colour Sergeant 'Tommy' Wall, who had been born and educated in barracks, enlisted as a boy bugler and knew virtually nothing of 'civvy street'. He was continually asking us questions about life outside and appeared really worried about going out after the war. However, I heard subsequently that he eventually died on the square at Eastney.

'After service in Egypt, Ceylon, Albania, Corfu and at Commachio and Argenta Gap, I eventually reached Exton, the 'ancestral home' which I had never seen before, in late summer 1945, prior to release.'

Stan Skippings – PO/X 4829, Continuous Service Squad 391

'I was a member of one of the first Continuous Service Squads who were sent to the RM Reserve Depot, Exton. We spent six weeks in the tented camp across the road from the main gate (now a car park and playing field). Our MTI was Sergeant Gerry Ball, a gentleman (as instructors went in those days) and I must say just like a father to us all. It was the most perfect six weeks, not a spot of rain, during which we carried out normal training during the forenoon and during the afternoon we worked on putting up defences all around the camp area. I and others of the squad were amongst the first to be 'confirmed' in the Camp Church by the Bishop of Exeter. We were all very sorry to leave Exton, and never more so than when we reached Portsmouth when after the peace and quiet of Devon we were greeted by an air raid which meant a nice march all the way to Eastney.'

Donald A Gibson MA M Ed – Rector of Berwickshire High School

'The civilian, who arrived at Exeter and was shunted down the branch to Woodbury Road, was in a far different situation from the modern recruit; certainly there was no chance of him backing out after a few days of unhappiness. The gates closed behind him and for good or ill he was in the Royal Marines. My turn came in July 1941 when all the Devon ways were lush with flowers; when the washing, which you so often seemed to do in cold water in zinc buckets, dried so readily in the endless still sunlight; when the pop music of the day featured an anxious mother and a daughter who wanted to go out dancing… that probably dates the period piece.

'Twenty fellows of varying provenance, thrown together in a barrack room, settled in easily enough in a world at war where your recruit training was the prelude to some real business on the battle fronts. Alone in my barrack room I had the benefit of a university education (in Classics of all things!) and after some dismay I had to set about forgetting it all and building bridges with my more practical companions who had all left school at fifteen. So I quietly suppressed the Classics degree… though in the unit to which I was first despatched the Commanding Officer, a Lieutenant Colonel RM, would never be persuaded that a Master of Arts might not necessarily be able to camouflage trucks. The Non-Commissioned Officers in charge of us probably regarded us with indulgent pity and taught us the wicked arts of boot-boning and blanco-ing and how to lay out our kits and keep the tormenting official-issue woolly vests rolled up for display.

'Everything was new and slightly sinister; the inoculations at the sickbay where the most stalwart sporty types regularly fainted at the thought; the complications of carrying arms at various improbable positions and the excruciating decision of how to salute officers simultaneously approaching on port and starboard. At mealtimes a sort of family service was the rule and the division of the mass provender in the baking tins was usually left to me, not so much because of my reputation for fairness as that I could somehow contrive 'that fourteen men came out of one tin'. We laboured clumsily on the SA ranges on the perimeter of the camp, the sacks suspended to simulate German bodies (with the straw leaking). We were expected to approach with bloodcurdling fervour, using horrid imprecations that had never crossed my lips before (one excessively well brought up fellow from the Shires charged the dummy with a ringing 'Tally-ho'). You occupied your spot in the gym while the doors, open to the estuary, let in the warm summer air. Bees buzzed all round the camp, especially on Saturday and Sunday afternoons and men dozed or wrote letters home and Lympstone seemed very far from a world at war.

'But the finest part of it for me was the Parade Ground. Is it still where it was, I wonder? If anything made me a Royal, it was that. At first it was very terrible. You had the feeling of an omniscient eye coupled to a mouth like a maroon which could devastate the wretch who moved the tip of his nose. Morning parade was at first a series of trials and errors which diminished (but never completely) as newer squads replaced our more blasé ones. Afternoon parade held for me a dreadful temptation. At 1400 we formed up; at 1403 on the other side of the Exe the 'Cornish Riviera Express' rattled down past Powderham Castle and I did so want to see it, for the Great Western had been a mystery to me till then. I once dared to look and actually got away with it. Then weeks later came the day when the band was marshalled and we marched behind it, we the mere civilians, privileged, shall I say, to swing our arms and to inherit several hundred years of tradition. It made a mark on me from which I have never recovered.

'And all this was Lympstone, I can see fellows lying on their beds darning their socks or out dhobying in the sunlight. I can hear their voices, name their names, but I don't know what became of them. In the drafting none of my barrack room went my way to the abortive Beach Unit and then 47 Commando, one of the originals. But when my six and a half years were up and I was latterly a Lieutenant RN in the RN School of Music at Burford, they were generous enough to put on a dinner for me at my departure; I made a speech and I guarantee that there was no one that day so 100% for the Corps than I was.'

Reg Watson

Reg Watson's view of Dalditch was as a 'Hell Hole', his first three weeks being spent in a Holding Battalion in Triangle Lines:

'We were issued with three brown, hairy, flea-ridden blankets and a pillowcase. The beds were made of wood, just six inches off the concrete floor, and the inside of the Nissen hut was red with rust, and condensation running down the walls. After three weeks of coal fatigues, washing slimy pots, peeling mountains of spuds, digging ditches, building the 500 yard range with pick and shovel, we moved to Hayes Lines for continuance of our basic training. We were allowed one fire at night... when it went out that was it. On our third day of training it started to rain, day after day, so you stepped out of your hut into four inches of Devon mud. Our dining hall was 200 yards through the rain and mud, with our knife, fork, spoon and mug.

'Breakfast consisted of two slices of bread, a one-inch square of margarine that tasted like axle grease and a dollop of something given to you on a tin plate... it could be rissoles, or a pre-fried, warmed up sausage with a spoonful of beans, or corned beef with a spoonful of mashed spuds and one that even I could not face – 'mechanised kippers'. This was warmed up 'herrings in tomato sauce'. This little gem came up twice a week, you either ate it or waited until dinner time.

'The dinners were beyond description, ninety percent of it finished up in the 'gash bin'. For tea, just read two slices of bread, one inch cube of margarine and a mug of tea. Jam you say? You'd be lucky.

'When our banquet was over, each man was responsible for washing his tin plate, which was done in the filthiest way I have ever seen anywhere in the world. Two old fashioned galvanised baths, filled with warm water, were placed outside the Dining Hall with one slimy dish cloth. In this you washed your plate; the water was never changed.

'The washing facilities were 'five-star' hotel treatment; about forty men were allocated to a wash hut which contained twenty five galvanised bowls. It was a fight of the fittest to get a wash bowl, to wash and shave in freezing cold water. To take a shower was an experience never to be forgotten. The showers were built on a hill with a twelve inch gap at the bottom of the iron sheet and an eighteen inch gap where it met the roof, you stood on a concrete floor awaiting the tepid water, and the wind howled and blew until you ended up with goose-pimples on top of your goose-pimples.

'Mr Perrett has mentioned one attraction called 'The Dalditch Dog". Whole companies of men would go down with dysentery, lasting up to a week. The latrines were just Elsan-type buckets, placed in a row inside a flat roof hut, privacy was nil, every man knew what each other was doing, because you sat next to each other. A large drum of sawdust was always at your disposal to cover up the filth; the stench could not be covered. After dark you were in real trouble, because they had no lights so we chose the surrounding countryside. To dispose of this, the permanent staff had a volunteer force of Pioneers who received sixpence per day extra, today that is two and a half pence. When I think back, they were either nutcases or they deserved the Victoria Cross.

'Before closing I must mention the immortal 'haversack ration', which was issued if you were away for the day shooting at Straight Point, or at Woodbury Common for field training, or on a twenty-five mile march. It was a gourmet's delight, consisting of two slices of bread with a one inch square of axle grease spread very thin and in the middle a delicious slice of fatty corned beef and that was it, nothing more until you returned to camp.

'That was a little bit of Dalditch Camp. If such conditions existed today there would be no Corps, or it would have its first mutiny. I can think of a glowing epitaph that should have been flown when the squads left for various drafts: *Through these portals passed the toughest, fittest men in the world.* We had to be … to survive this Hell Hole called Dalditch.

'If you young Marines think you have it hard: just thank your lucky stars that Dalditch is now a ghost camp… with all its memories.'

C Waters

'Lympstone. I arrived at Lympstone on 17 December 1942, one of the four 'elder' members of my squad. I remember, with gratitude, the bandsmen who stayed back over Christmas to entertain us and help those who felt homesick to get over their troubles.

'Our first instructor was a Corporal who was very popular, but he came 'unstuck' and was replaced by Colour Sergeant 'Nobby' Clark. This change was not very popular at the time, but the squad soon came to realise that the new instructor was a friend. Mr Gibson mentions the Parade Ground, but he did not mention the 'double' with the Band playing *Keel Row*, or something similar. As the weeks progressed, so did the amount of equipment that was loaded on to your person. This was alright until it was your turn to wear Full Marching Order, and then the double became a shambles. Not so for Colour Sergeant Clark. He took so long in inspecting the equipment and how it should be worn that we missed the shambles!

'What a picture! We had been issued with a kitbag containing various items of clothing, including three undershirts, flannel, white, Admiralty pattern – all the same size – with your number stamped across the tail. Imagine thirty chaps, some tall, some short, some fat, some thin, each wearing his flannel undershirt. No wonder a roar of laughter went up.

'Dalditch. I agree it was grim, but not quite as bad as portrayed by Mr Watson – or was I more philosophical? In winter the mud was deep and in summer that dust was thick. As an instructor, Mr Watson should know that finding a 'dirty' rifle was easier than pinching toffee from a kid. As to the blankets, they were a disgrace. Venereal Disease was unknown, but Impetigo was rife. Washing-up facilities? Well, it is remarkable what a little RM ingenuity could do. The grub was not brilliant, but was not that bad, unless the cook b******* up the bully beef by turning it into rissoles – a sure winner for Dalditch Dog!

'I became a Lance Corporal, adjudged top of that class. The Colour Sergeant Instructor did not agree with this – he disliked any man that received pay from his employers. He had been recalled from a job with NAAFI. I have always envied his exhibition of rapid fire, every movement so cool and deliberate.'

William Scott

'Reg Watson was lucky not going to Dalditch when I did, under canvas, receiving sixpence per day for Living-under-Canvas Allowance, a magnificent addition to the ten shillings per week pay.

'I was at Exton, which was actually far superior to Butlin's Holiday Camp, in late September and October, wonderful summer weather in glorious Devon, for six or seven weeks of basic training. We were told we had to get in as much instruction in that time as would have occupied twelve or eighteen months in peacetime.

'We marched to Dalditch to join up with the 8th Battalion and the weather changed for the worse that very day. My heart sank as we paraded on a muddy field and I had my first sight of Regimental Sergeant Major Keble, known as 'The Bull'. He put the fear of God in me, but I learned to admire and respect and virtually love the man for his whole-hearted dedication to the Corps. A magnificent type and, like the rest of the long-serving NCOs, the backbone of the service.

'We were under canvas, five to a tent, on duckboards. Winter had set in and the place was a quagmire. No electricity, no toilets, no running water, no anything. To walk across a muddy field, wash and shave, by touch, in the dark, in cold water, except for the stubs of candles taken by the experienced… well, I could go on, but we survived and built Dalditch.

'I remember the completion of the Nissen huts and those beautiful beds Reg Watson complains about. This was four-star treatment, like moving from a doss house to a Hilton Hotel.

'I spent a winter there, conditions improving all the time and reached a stage of physical fitness never achieved before or since. We were wolves and tigers, but magnificently trained and disciplined wolves and tigers. The comradeship was terrific, English, Scots, Welsh, Irish, from all walks of life, and every county in Britain and no matter how grim the position, there was always some wit to crack a joke.

'I think it was April and we were looking forward to summer in Dalditch, but it was over, and we were en route for Llanion barracks in Pembroke dock, the place that God forgot. But the less said about that the better.

'We always talked about going back to Devon and dear old Dalditch, but for many of those marvellous chaps, it was only a dream. We left Pembroke to form 41 Commando in Troon, and Salerno was to end the dreams for a lot of the finest specimens of manhood, and the best friends I have ever had.

'Whenever I think of the Royal Marines and I think and talk of them very, very often, I think of Dalditch and say: *thank God for the Royal Marines and thank God for Dalditch*'.

'Sadly, it took a war to make them both happen to me.'

Anonymous Globe and Laurel *Report*

'Scorriton Down, on the edge of the moor above Buckfastleigh provided a four day break from barrack life for the recruits post WW2, and depending on the weather it was either a welcome tonic or a nightmare experience. Whilst some returned to Lympstone sunburnt and blistered, one recounts, 'We have cowered, at 0200 hours, in a hedgerow with forty recruits under groundsheets during a thunderstorm; we have stood in eighteen inches of water in slit trenches on Down Ridge, silent and 'chokker', with rivers pouring down our necks, waiting for Captain Hill's 'bangs' to go off; and we've squelched across the moors after twelve hours work, to find tents blown flat and the galley fire trenches acting as canals for all the water in the Dart.

'In the 11th week of training the Company organises the platoons into a four-day cycle, one day each for travelling to and from Scorriton Down, and two for training. Tents and all stores are taken to the down and laid out on the camp site. The platoon leaves Lympstone at 1000 in full marching order, going by train via Exeter to South Brent, and then by rapid road march about seventeen miles to camp. Following two days of intensive field work, day and night firing, the platoon marches off at 0600 on the final day, again in marching order, the eleven miles to Totnes station to entrain for Lympstone. There is a proud boast that Scorriton is never cancelled, whatever the weather; Scorriton tests you, in weapon handling, field craft, in determination to overcome difficulties, in endurance, guts and self discipline.'

Whatever the weather!

Major D R Christie-Miller

'I joined the Royal Marines at ITCRM on 1 May 1962. It was a warm late spring day and the black and green huts of the camp were embedded neatly and tidily in between well-tended gardens. We clambered down from the three tonners at the Stone Block, now demolished without requiem and stone blocks in name only and I recall looking out of my cabin window, across the parade to where I could catch a glimpse of other newcomers and other huts.

'My experience of huts is limited – a few weeks as a cadet and my time as a Young Officer but the huts made a lasting impact. They had many fine qualities and not a few faults, but on balance I believe they did a better job that the vinyl coated, hollow doored, glassed towers in which we incarcerate our recruits these days.

The last remaining wooden hut at CTCRM, Lympstone

'Let me convince you.

'A hut was a *hut* – not an accommodation block. A hut was a home with a heart and a hearth. And what a hearth. A coke burning stove squatted in the middle surrounded by white painted bricks. Coke would be collected in sandbags and carefully stored in the scuttle. In summer it seemed an indecency, occupying space without a purpose, but when winter came it took its rightful place – a throbbing, demanding epicentre, a focal point.

'The other focal point was the NCO's individual cabin. It had privacy and gave the occupant a sanctuary. But a roofless sanctuary and most of what was said in the hut could be heard, and vice versa. There were many stentorian cries to 'Pipe down' or 'Who's going to polish my brasses then?' Beds weren't beds either. They were the bottom half of a two-tier metal bunk with appropriate prongs at each corner. You had a bedspace, with a small rug sometimes, but more often than not polished and cold lino. Lockers were wood. Mainly unadorned inside, but an occasional photograph was propped up on a shelf in a plain gilt frame from Woolworths. There was enough room for your kit – just.

'The kit was black, white, green, khaki and demanding. The changes in fashions were reflected on the cleaning trellises that squatted under the corrugated iron walkways in between and at the back of the huts. White blanco, green blanco, black polish, Brasso and Duraglit stains all competed for space on the wooden slats.

'If you stood there for a few moments a steady stream of men would pass you on their way to the bathrooms and heads. They all carried their own set of gear including, if they were wise, a plug for the basin. The bathrooms were designed to clean a large number of men in a short time – rows of basins, all plug-less, a wall of mirrors, taps that gushed water, and showers that worked in vast, steaming gulps.

'There were other huts too. The cold, breeze block Mansards, some of which still stand, laagered together as though for their own protection. They had their own signature as well – noisy metal window frames that would announce the end of a day's work when shut by a departing incumbent.

'Then there were the office huts – and now only one remains. You tried to ignore them but on occasions they beckoned – you'd stamp up the brick stairs, peer at your boots and notice the dust and dead leaves through the cracks in the floor, pull down your battledress blouse, finger your beret and peer hastily into the Adjutant's office, your report fluttering in your hand. There was always someone in his office and you always had to wait, saluting and being saluted. Then knock, 'come in', and enter for interrogation. On leaving you'd hurry down the steps and probably ruin the polish on your boots by stumbling over the ill-sited boot scraper set, probably for that purpose only, by the entrance.

'At nights the huts hunched their shoulders and waited for their regular callers, the wandering patrol – a trained soldier and a recruit at ten paces distance, the Officer of the Day (OOD) and the Duty SNCO.

"You take the right side, Sergeant and I'll meet you at the gym."

A King's Squad marches out of the main gate

'You rattled the doorknobs, pulled, pushed and hoped they wouldn't open, peered through the window at the Imprest Officer's safe, sitting in the glow of a purposefully lit lamp and slowly made your way down the long dormant black lines.

'I would like to see that one last remaining block, wooden hut on the main camp road at CTCRM preserved. I like it. To me it's got the same qualities as the gap in Terry Thomas' teeth – intangible but positive. I would like to see it turned into a museum. Not a paying one or a proper museum but a small memorial to the history of ITCRM and CTCRM. It also might take the eye away from that piece of sculpture. I see it containing photographs, uniforms, items of kit and a visitors' book for use by retired and returning Royal Marines only. You come to see your son's King's Squad pass out and pop in on your way to the parade ground; you sign the book, turn a few pages and discover the address of long forgotten squad mates, behind you a Bren gun sits on the floor, and on the wall hangs a black pack: its straps gleaming like wet liquorice. What year was that? 1956? Well, step out into the present day but look back at that hut. It helped make you what you are.'

*

Note: The hut in question does not fulfil Major Christie-Miller's dream unfortunately, but is put to good use by the Royal Marine Reservists now, and the piece of sculpture to which he refers ('Both Arms') has since been transferred to Poole and was replaced by the new RM Commando sculpture on 20 September 1986.

Colonel R I McGarel-Groves

'As a member of the January 1939 batch of Probationary Second Lieutenants, I joined Exton in June 1940 from Depot Deal; those with cars made their own way whilst the remainder piled into an East Kent bus: and a thirty hundredweight truck took our baggage.

'We were accommodated in eleven Bell tents (two per tent) in a double row at the edge of the wood, on that area which became the old Officers' Mess vegetable garden. The Mess was in use, and two accommodation huts were partially in use (we were allowed in to use the showers) and as work progressed we moved into the one nearest the wood sometime late June or July, after which the tents were struck. In fine weather life under canvas was quite pleasant, but when it rained these tents leaked and despite little ditches around each, things got pretty damp. We had all been issued with camp equipment, so we slept on camp beds and washed using little canvas bowls supported on a tripod. You filled these from the canvas bucket, and you hung your clothes on the folding canvas chair. We wore Khaki Service Dress with puttees and a peaked cap initially, but it was a welcome relief when we were issued with Khaki Battledress. (Our blue uniforms and mess kit remained in uniform trunks).

'Our Military Instructor was Colonel Jerram: who had won the DSO at Gallipoli as quite a young officer and he gave us enthralling lectures on the first landing, so vivid that you could almost imagine you were there; but our course started with a disadvantage of trying to teach First World War tactics, as improved between the wars, at a time when a totally different sort of war seemed to be gripping Europe. I can remember a splendid Tactical Exercise Without Troops, lasting two days, on the siting of a bivouac area when the importance of watering animals downstream was stressed... I wonder how many of us had to put this problem into practice for real?

'Only two failed the course, losing a month's seniority; the remainder went to sea, and of the original twenty two, seven were killed and two became Prisoners of War.

*

Note: As a Captain, he commanded No 4 Guard (ITCRM) at the Trooping the Colour ceremony 6 May 1955, pictured on page 12.

Young officers study tactical situations

Appendices

Appendix A

Globe and Laurel References

In addition to the progress reports in the journal throughout the war years as RM Reserve Depot (Devon) was built up, the following references will assist in tracing further developments up to the present.

Year	*Page*	
1947	20	Between 1000 and 1500 recruits undergoing Group II training
	186	Men clear snow, sand, and anti-invasion obstacles
	260–3	Aerial view of original camp and first post-war 'Open Day'
	298	Some statistics, including rations consumed
1948	150 & 176	The first National Service recruits arrive for seventeen-week
1950	176	course
1951	22 & 61	First King's Birthday Parade, and Band departs
		Mar (80): Officer's Wing formed – direct entry
	177	Single-tier beds and wardrobes arrive
1952	115	Open Day
1953	41	Officers' School moves in from Stonehouse (Plymouth)
1954	31	School Entry Courses
		BBC broadcasts from camp theatre ('Brains Trust' and 'Variety Ahoy' with Bob Monkhouse, Charlie Chester and Pearl Carr)
1955	171	Captain General visits and receives green beret
1956	221 & 271	Further BBC broadcasts made
		Searchlight Tattoo held over five days
	81	St Albans Church rebuilding, Commando school leaves
1957	190	Small Arms School moves in from Browndown (Gosport)
1958	137 & 186	Help Yourself service introduced in Dining Hall
1959	252–3	First Junior Entry Squad arrives
		Sergeants' Mess improvements
1960	89	Commando specialised training
	150–1	Commando Training and Non-Commissioned Officer Training Wing moves in
1961	8–9	Training details
	171	Redevelopment plans (in five stages) announced
	312–3	23,000 attend Searchlight Tattoo

1962	9	Royal Artillery arrive to form 29 Commando Battery
	82	Royal Artillery Training
1963	163	'What's going on at ITCRM' (alterations)
	234	The first new accommodation block opening 12 July by Commandant General
1964	43	Four new accommodation blocks, two Company Offices, the Light Air Detachment and Motor Transport Unit Workshop now in use
	397	New Sports Pavilion opened (named after Captain Easterbrook), and Tercentenary Display
1965	296	Lieutenant Colonel C E Vaughan OBE (Commanding Officer of Achnacarry) at 820 Squad green beret presentation
1966	371	Aerial view and map; eighth barrack block planned
1967	389	Two King's Squads pass out together (862 & 863)
1968	153	Exmouth adopts the Corps
1969	110–1	Opening of new Stores building
1971	165	Commandant General lays foundation stone of new training complex (26 April)
1972	78–9	A new look in New Entry Training
	212–3	Training foreign troops
	338	Commando Training Centre trains all three services and (344–5) Junior Command Course
1974	96–8	Changes to twenty-four week adult syllabus
	226-7	Young Officers' training
	286–7	Two King's Squads pass out together (58 and 59 Troop)
	338	Normandy Block (Junior Entries) opening
1975	32	Modernisation progress
	160	Commandant General change over at Commando Training Centre
1976	26–7	Further alterations to Commando Training Centre
	92–3	Railway station under construction and old Sergeants' Mess pictured
	146	'Awayday Special' – the railway comes to Lympstone Commando
1978	107	The new Physical and Recreational Training Complex under construction
1979	20	New sports Hall and Swimming Pool open
	222–3	Physical Training School moves in from Deal
	290	Command training for Senior and Junior NCOs

1980	54	Picture of new Sergeants' Mess
	144–5	HRH Prince Andrew earns his green beret
1981	160	The new church of St Alban
1983	203	HRH Prince Edward undertakes the potential officers course and (275) joins the Corps 5 September (Young Officers' course started 10 September 1986)
1984	228–9	The Falklands Hall (main presentation centre) opened by Major General Sir Jeremy Moore KCB OBE MC
	382–3	Report on the fifteen weeks' training for recruits, and TV personality from 'Blue Peter' (Peter Duncan) trains with 184 Troop
1985	241–4	Princess of Wales' visit (25 July)
1986	293	Royal Marines Commando Memorial unveiled.

*

Appendix B

Local Press Reports

Exmouth Journal

1 July 1939	Mentions the possibility of a Depot for National Training in the Littleham area, and the land plus services required are being considered.
29 July 1939	The choice of Littleham is abandoned and Exton being considered.
12 August 1939	Exton confirmed as the choice.
10 November 1945	Dalditch Camp staff entertain nearly 300 townswomen at a special open day at the camp in appreciation for their work in the various forces canteens etc throughout the war.

Express and Echo

22 July 1939	States that the Littleham site was not suitable for the Royal Marines, and that Exmouth would have been happy to have them there.
23 July 1939	Refers to negotiations at Exton for RM Special Reserves.
25 March 1961	A modern barracks is to be built on the site of the old temporary wartime camp, as ITCRM Lympstone

Note: the newspaper's wartime files were destroyed in air raids

Successful recruits receive their green berets, and the best man of the squad is awarded the King's Badge

The outstanding Young Officer receives the Sword of Honour

Appendix C

A Brief History of the Nutwell Court Estate

Researched by Robert Ridding

Apart from the fact that Lympstone Camp was built on part of this estate, there is another link through the Corps' Gibraltar connection (Gibraltar being the single battle honour shown in their badge).

Lieutenant General George Augustus Eliott arrived on the Rock on 25 May 1777 and as Governor of the garrison he weathered the greatest of several sieges Gibraltar experienced, and as an experienced engineer was responsible for much of the fortification. Born on Christmas Day in 1717 he married Anne, daughter of the last Sir Francis Drake of Buckland Abbey in 1748, and before his death in 1790 he was elevated to the title Lord Heathfield, Baron of Gibraltar. Through the Drake connection one of his family estates became Nutwell Court, and his son, the second Lord Heathfield, a General in the Army, was responsible for many alterations to this house in 1796. Upon his death in 1813 the title became extinct, but his sister married John Trayton Fuller of Ashdown Park, and their third son Thomas assumed the surname of Eliott-Drake that same year, and in 1821 he was created a baronet.

The family line continued at Nutwell until the last member sold the land which now comprises the camp in 1940 for the Royal Marine Militia. Captain Meyrick who was the person concerned died the following year, and the remainder of the estate was acquired by Mr G V Northcott who was not related to the original family.

Nutwell has the distinction of having been recorded in the Domesday Book, William the Conqueror's 'census' completed in 1086. This tells that prior to 1066 the manor was owned by one called Donne, presumably a Saxon, and that in 1086 Donne was still in occupation, which is quite rare as normally Saxon Landlords were deprived of their manors to be given as rewards to William's Norman friends. In primitive times no house of merit could be built except where there was a plentiful supply of fresh water, and this is true of Nutwell, as the name implies. The 'Nut' part presumably applied to the nut trees which grew near the well or to Nota its first owner.

The first stone castle built here was by the Dinham family in the Fourteenth Century; they had arrived in this country with the Conqueror from Dinant in Brittany and at first settled in North Devon before acquiring Nutwell.

During the War of the Roses in 1459 the Earl of March (later King Edward IV) and the Earls of Warwick and Salisbury took refuge at Nutwell when forced to flee the country, until their host Sir John Dinham smuggled them out from Exmouth by boat to

France. Then when the King returned to claim his throne, Sir John was rewarded with large areas of Devon, and appointed to a high office; now he pulled down his castle and built in its place an elegant manor house.

The direct Dinham line died out in the late Fifteenth Century and the property was sold by one of the daughters to Sir John Prideaux, Sergeant-at-Law. This family held Nutwell through four generations and were buried in the chapel there, and the monument to them now seen in Woodbury Church was probably removed there from the chapel before Amias Prideaux sold out to Sir Henry Ford in the reign of Charles II (1660–86).

In 1646 during the civil war, Nutwell was occupied by the 'Roundheads', and then in 1685 the estate was bought by Sir Henry Pollexfen, a barrister of the Inner Temple, and later Lord Chief Justice of Common Pleas. It was his son Henry who, by marrying in 1699, brought the property into the Drake family, as his wife Gertrude was the sister of Sir Francis Drake (the fourth baronet) who was descended from the famous Admiral… and so it continued in that line until 1941.

LITTLEHAM CAMP PROJECT ABANDONED.

Will Royal Marine Militia Go to Exton?

SITE MORE ACCESSIBLE.

The project to establish a camp for eight hundred officers and men of the Special Reserve, Royal Marines, on Woodlands and Westdown Farms, Littleham, has been abandoned.

NOVEL ESTABLISHMENT.

The camp, which was to have been the only one of its kind in the country, was to consist of hutments for the accommodation of men of Militia age who were accepted for service with the Royal Marines.

Conferences were held with Exmouth Urban Council representatives over the question of the making of roads and the provision of services, but it is understood that in the end the site was not considered to be as accessible as was required, while it would have been necessary for the men in training there to travel some two miles to Exmouth docks in order to get at the craft in which they would obtain some of their tuition in seamanship.

NOVEL ESTABLISHMENT.

Negotiations, it is stated, have since been opened with the object of establishing the camp near Nutwell House, the Exeside seat of the Drake family. It is understood that the Admiralty regard the establishment of the camp as a matter of urgency, and representatives direct from Whitehall have been conducting the negotiations in the district.

At one time it was hoped to begin preliminary work on the camp at Nutwell next week, but difficulties appear to have arisen, and it may be that yet another site will have to be sought.

Capt. R. O. Meyrick, of Nutwell Court, has stated that he has no knowledge of the site on which such a camp would be established. He added that he had been approached in the matter, but that, so far as he was concerned, it would go no farther.

The news of the abandonment of the camp project for Littleham will be received with mixed feelings in the Exmouth district. There were numbers of people who held that the presence of troops would not be an advantage to the town from the point of view of a seaside residential resort, but, on the other hand, the majority probably felt that the spending power of a fairly considerable body of men, quartered in the town all the year round, would give an impetus to local business, particularly during the winter months.

ROYAL MARINES TO CAMP AT EXTON.

Admiralty Order to Proceed with Work.

MR. CEDRIC DREWE AND AGRICULTURAL INTERESTS.

The Admiralty have finally decided to establish the permenant camp for the militia of the Royal Marines on the Nutwell Court Estate at Exton.

The decision was conveyed in the course of a letter to Mr. Cedric Drewe, M.P. for the Honiton Division. Mr. Drewe is Parliamentary Private Secretary to the Minister of Agriculture (Sir Reginald Dorman-Smith), and had endeavoured to induce the Admiralty in the interests of local agriculture to adopt an alternative camp. As already reported in the "Exmouth Journal," there were negotiations for a site on Woodlands Farm, Littleham.

The camp will be designed to accommodate nine hundred officers and men.

ADMIRALTY DECISION.

Capt. Austin Hudson, Civil Lord of the Admiralty, who sent the letter conveying the Admiralty decision to Mr. Drewe, states that the representations made have been given careful and sympathetic consideration, but it has been found impossible to secure an equally suitable location in the neighbourhood.

The letter is as follows:

"As I promised when we met in my room last week, arrangements were immediately made to look at any alternative sites the local representative of the Ministry of Agriculture might be able to suggest, as well as the two sites that were suggested by a firm of local estate agents and mentioned at the meeting.

"The officials of your Ministry have been most helpful, and I understand that their local representative has thoroughly searched the estuary of the Exe on both sides for any possible sites that would avoid interference with agricultural interests, but without success. The only site suggested to us is one of lower agricultural value on the same estate, but this particular land is admittedly better farmed than the Exton land, so that the net difference does not appear to be very substantial.

BAD APPROACHES.

"This alternative site has been inspected by three of the Admiralty officers who were at the meeting, and they report that, although in itself it is a fair site, the drawbacks connected with its location and approaches are considerable.

"Although it is within 1½ miles of the estuary, the approaches to it are narrow and steep Devonshire lanes with high hedges. One of the quite unsuited for motor traffic, and the other would have to be widened before the construction of the camp could be started. There is no outfall for the purified sewage effluent near the site, and the disposal of this would be a difficult problem.

A GUN BATTERY.

"The site is on the crest of a hill about 200 feet above the river level, and is very exposed for an all-the-year camp. Access to the river for boat practice would be most inconvenient, and would involve crossing the main Exter-Exmouth road. The boat station would, of course, be entirely isolated instead of under observation, as at Exton.

"Apart from the necessity of having a sea or river view for the gun battery, some importance is attached to the camp being in close proximity to the water, for psychological reasons, as the camp is for training Royal Marines.

"WINKLE INTERESTS!"

"The other two sites were also inspected, but were found to be quite impossible, being too steeply undulating in small enclosures, in addition to disadvantages similar to those attending the Gulliford site.

"In these circumstances, while regretting the interference with agricultural interests, I do not feel justified in accepting the serious drawbacks that would be entailed by giving up the Exton site in favour of either of the alternatives mentioned. I am satisfied that no harm should come to the fishing or winkle interests, by reason of the proposal.

"After careful consideration I have, therefore, given instructions to proceed with the construction of the camp at Exton."

PREMATURE STATEMENT.

Mr. E. P. Newton, of Chard, agent to the Nutwell Estate, writes as follows:—

With reference to he letter from the Civil Lord of the Admiralty to Mr. Cedric Drewe, M.P. for Honiton, it is desired to state that nothing was previously known by the owner, Capt. Meyrick, or myself, as his agent, of the inspection by the Admiralty of any alternative site forming part of the Nutwell Estate.

CAMPS AT EXMOUTH.

Several thousand infantrymen, artillerymen, and engineers, will be in training in the Exmouth district during the coming fortnight, and camps are already being prepared at Veiges, St. Johns Road; Four Beeches, at the Blackhill end of the same road; and at Dalditch.

Newspaper extracts from the *Exmouth Journal* (29 July and 12 August 1939)

Aerial view of Lympstone, 1986

1942

DAILY ROUTINE

Time	*Bugle Call*	*Remarks*
0600	Reveille	Sundays at 0700
0645		Rooms to be clean and beds made up
0700	Men's 2nd Meal Call	Breakast (Sundays at 0800)
0730	Warning for Parade	
0745	Sick Call Quarter Call	Sick parade in the Drill Shed (Sundays at 0830)
0755	Markers	
0800	Fall In	Squads fall in on parade unless otherwise ordered
1300	Dismiss	
1305	Action, followed by one 'G'	Passive Air Defence Watch muster in the Drill Shed. (Saturdays and Sundays at (1205)
1315	Men's 2nd Meal Call	Dinner (Saturdays and Sundays at (1230)
1345	Warning for Parade	
1315	Sick Call	Sick Parade in the Drill Shed
1410	Markers	
1415	Fall In	
1700	Dismiss	
1705	Men's 2nd Meal Call	Tea
1745	Sick Call	Sick Parade in the Drill Shed
1800	Defaulters	Extra parades
1930	Men's 2nd Meal Call	Supper
2215	Lights Out	Lights to be switched out in rooms
FRIDAYS ONLY:—		
1200		Depot Staff fall in for payment
1350	Fall In	Miss-musters and recruits fall in for payment
SUNDAYS ONLY:—		
0730	Holy Communion	
0830	Fatigues	
0930	R.C. Service	
1000	Fall In	Church of England and other denominations fall in

NOTE:—Read Depot Daily Orders on your Company Notice Board for alterations to daily routine

1986

A typical day might go something like this:

0600	Reveille	Get up, shower, shave, strip and remake bed, sweep out bed space, sweep and polish the room, remove rubbish.
0630	Breakfast	After breakfast draw weapons.
0700	Prepare for first parade	Clean teeth and carry out room and floor duties. Check kit for period one and make sure the kit required for the rest of the day is ready for use in the locker. Check cleanliness of your weapon. Dress for first parade. Lock your locker. Final check of room. Check yourself in the mirror. Muster on parade ground.
0730	Parade	
0800–0845	Period 1	Drill on parade ground.
0845–0940	Period 2	Map-reading lecture in training block.
0950–1035	Period 3	Practical exercise on the playing fields.
1035–1055	Stand Easy	(Tea break)
1055–1140	Period 4	Physical training in gymnasium.
1150–1235	Period 5	Weapon training with SLR.
1235–1355	Lunch	
1355–1440	Period 6	Live-firing SLR on 25-metre range.
1450–1535	Period 7	Map-reading exercise on Woodbury Common.
1545–1630	Period 8	Map-reading continued.
1635–1730		Return to Camp. Clean and return stores.
1745	Supper	
1800–2000		Clean and prepare gear for next day.
2230	Lights out	

Daily routines from 1942 and 1986